CONTENTS

Chapter One: The Problems of Waste

Chapter Two: Reducing Waste

Introduction

Waste Pollution is the fifty-seventh volume in the **Issues** series. The aim of this series is to offer up-to-date information about important issues in our world.

Waste Pollution examines the issues of waste and its management, including recycling, reuse and the reduction of waste.

The information comes from a wide variety of sources and includes:
Government reports and statistics
Newspaper reports and features
Magazine articles and surveys
Web site material
Literature from lobby groups
and charitable organisations.

It is hoped that, as you read about the many aspects of the issues explored in this book, you will critically evaluate the information presented. It is important that you decide whether you are being presented with facts or opinions. Does the writer give a biased or an unbiased report? If an opinion is being expressed, do you agree with the writer?

Waste Pollution offers a useful starting-point for those who need convenient access to information about the many issues involved. However, it is only a starting-point. At the back of the book is a list of organisations which you may want to contact for further information.

*****

Waste – what's the problem?

Information from www.useitagain.org.uk

What is waste?

Together, we produce around 27 million tonnes of household waste in the UK every year. That's a massive half a tonne per person.

Our household waste is made up of a number of different materials. Listed in order of weight, these are:

- 32% paper and card
- 21% organic/food
- 10% other
- 9% glass
- 7% dust
- 6% ferrous metal (steel or 'tin' cans etc.)
- 6% hard plastic
- 5% plastic film
- 2% non-ferrous metal (aluminium cans etc.)
- 2% textiles

Source: Environment Agency

According to Wastewatch, we can recover 50% or more of household waste through reuse or by recycling, but we only recycle about 10% or just less than 3 million tonnes of it. So what happens to the remaining 24 million tonnes of unrecycled household waste, and why is it such a problem?

Tip: More than 50% of our household waste is recyclable but we only recycle 10%.

Why is waste a problem?

Every year in the UK, 27 million tonnes of household waste needs to be disposed of in some way by our local waste disposal authorities. Unfortunately, this waste does not simply disappear into thin air, and this is an issue for all of us. Waste disposal by any method has environmental and cost implications. When waste is disposed of instead of being reused or recycled, raw materials have to be used to make new products. The production of goods from raw materials has a greater environmental impact and costs more.

Tip: Each year 22 million tonnes of household waste is dumped in landfill sites.

Getting rid of waste

There are currently two main methods of getting rid of waste. These are landfill and incineration.

Landfill

Every year, 22 million tonnes (81% of our household waste) are put in landfill sites. Waste is dumped into either large holes in the ground (these can be natural or resulting from quarrying or mining) or piled up into artificial hills. There are several major drawbacks to disposing of waste in this way, although to counteract these effects today's landfills are constructed and operated to very high standards. The drawbacks:

- Chemicals, heavy metals and bacteria can leak into the soil and underground water table
- Organic waste in particular can cause problems by degrading to form leachate – a highly polluting liquid
- Degradation in landfill sites also produces methane, which is a 'greenhouse' gas which adds to global warming. A build-up of methane gas locally can also cause explosions
- Some materials such as glass and plastics do not easily break down
- Most sites are far away from the large towns where the household waste was originally produced. This means high transportation costs and of course more fossil fuel use and pollution.

EC Landfill Directive

A new law will soon come into effect which forces all EC countries to considerably reduce the amount and types of waste that is landfilled (EC Landfill Directive). Currently, 81% of our household waste goes into landfill sites. By the year 2020, we will be legally obliged by the Directive to reduce this to 35%.

Incineration

- Incineration is not waste-free and also has drawbacks. Up to 10% of the incinerated waste becomes

'bottom ash'. The bottom ash is itself disposed of in landfill sites
- 5% of the incinerated waste becomes 'fly ash' and has to be disposed of as hazardous waste
- There is public concern about incineration.

Tip: Reduce waste by reusing old jam jars, biscuit tins and scrap paper.

The drawbacks of making new products from raw materials.

In some cases, using raw materials instead of recycled material to make new products creates a much greater environmental impact and has a higher cost.

Activities such as mining and extraction, quarrying and logging can be destructive to the natural environment and local wildlife. The energy required to make new products out of raw materials can be more than that needed to make products out of recycled material.

Household waste and recycling

In England and Wales, the amount of household waste increased by around a third in total, and by almost 26 per cent per person, between 1983/4 and 1999/2000. During 1999/2000 over 26 million tonnes (an average of almost 500kg per person) was collected by local authorities. Just over 10 per cent of this waste is recycled or composted.

	Kilograms per person per year				
	1983/84	1991/92	1997/98	1998/99	1999/00
Waste not recycled	393	414	434	433	447
Waste recycled/composted	3	11	38	42	51
Total waste	397	425	472	475	498

Source: DEFRA. National Assembly for Wales, CIPFA

For example, aluminium (used in many drink cans) is made from bauxite ore. The extraction and production process is costly and environmentally damaging. But recycling aluminium instead of using raw materials makes an energy saving of more than 90%, cuts emissions by 99% and reduces import costs. It also saves on landfill space and reduces the need for incineration.

So what can we recycle?

About half our household waste is recyclable, yet on average, we only recycle around 10% of it. This rate is way below countries such as Germany and Sweden.

- The above information is from the web site www.useitagain.org.uk run by the Department for Environment, Food and Rural Affairs.

Top 10 wacky waste facts!

Information from Waste Watch

Have you ever thought about how much rubbish you and your family throw away every week? Or why we need to stop throwing so much away? I bet you haven't! This article is full of wacky waste facts and there's also lots for you to do.

1 We use over six billion glass bottles and jars each year. It would take you over three and a half thousand years to sing 'Six Billion Green Bottles'!

2 Every year we need a forest the size of Wales to provide all the paper we use in Britain.

3 Each year in Britain, we throw away 27 million tonnes of rubbish from home. This weighs the same as three and a half million double-decker buses. A queue of buses that long would go around the world one and a half times.

4 An average person throws away 74 kg of organic waste each year, which is the same as 1077 banana skins.

5 The amount of waste paper buried each year would fill 103,448 double-decker buses, which if parked nose to tail would go all the way from London to Milan.

6 Each year food shops give away enough carrier bags to cover the whole of London with a layer of bags.

7 Every day 80 million food and drinks cans end up in landfill (being buried) – that's one and a half cans per person. In a year, each person could fill a bath with the contents of these cans!

8 We fill about 300 million square metres of land with rubbish every year, that's the same as covering the pitch at Old Trafford, Manchester United Football Club's ground, 28,450 times. To walk around the pitch that many times would take you from midnight on 1st January until midday on May 5th!

9 One million tonnes of nappies are thrown away every year, that's 8 million nappies every day. Each child uses a total of 5850 nappies in their lifetime; that weights the same as an average family car!

10 In the 1950s the world made less than 5 million tonnes of plastic products. This has increased to about 80 million tonnes today. We produce and use 20 times more plastic today than we did 50 years ago!

- The above information is from Waste Watch's web site which can be found at www.wastewatch.org.uk Alternatively, see page 41 for their address details.

The mess we're in!

We are a nation addicted to chucking stuff out. But most of what we call waste could be used again by someone else.

How many worlds do we need?

If everyone in the world was as wasteful as we are in the UK we would need 8 worlds to keep going.

Garbage in – garbage out

At the heart of the problem is a relentless cycle of . . .

■ Over-production

Making so much new stuff, uses up the world's valuable natural resources. Logging and paper companies like Asia Pulp and Paper wreck rainforests. Elsewhere producers are damaging our peat bogs and degrading wildlife sites.

■ Bad practice

Using too many fossil fuels in the production process causes climate change. Factories and landfill pollute because companies put financial profit before good practice. Things aren't made to last so they need replacing prematurely.

■ Excessive disposal

The average person in the UK throws out their body weight in rubbish every 3 months. Most of this could be reprocessed but instead it is sent to incinerators or landfill.

Rather than tackle the problems through recycling and waste reduction, the Government burns and dumps our waste.

Incineration and landfill

Most of our waste is burned or buried which is bad for the environment and our health.

Incineration

The combustion of waste at high temperatures:

■ Encourages more waste

Incinerators need a minimum of rubbish to operate. To meet demand,

Friends of the Earth

local authorities are abandoning recycling and waste reduction plans.

■ Uses up energy

Even incinerators that generate electricity aren't an energy saving option. Recycling saves far more energy because it means making less new things from raw materials.

■ Causes pollution

Smoke, gases and ash from incinerators can contain harmful dioxins which are a cause of cancer.

Landfill

Dumping rubbish in the ground or in waste mountains:

■ Releases toxins

Rotting rubbish emits explosive gases and polluting liquids. Methane emissions contribute to climate change.

■ Threatens our quality of life

Landfill creates problems for local communities. Nuisances include more traffic, noise, odours, smoke, dust, litter and pests.

From bad to worse . . .

European laws are forcing the Government to reduce landfilled waste. The £400 million a year they raise from landfill taxes could be used to provide every home in the UK with a recycling collection service, composting and more . . .

Instead the Government is:

■ Replacing landfill with incinerators.
■ Dumping toxic incineration ash in existing landfill.

Friends of the Earth says:

■ Don't build any more incinerators.
■ Use money from landfill taxes for recycling and waste reduction.

■ The above information is from Friends of the Earth's web site which can be found at www.foe.co.uk

© *Friends of the Earth*

Waste facts

Are you doing your bit?

Metals (e.g. food and drink cans)

- Every year in the UK we use 13 billion steel cans which, placed end to end, would stretch to the moon – three times!
  (Source: Steel Can Recycling Information Bureau)
- Producing steel from recycled materials saves 75 per cent of the energy needed to make steel from virgin materials.
  (Source: Steel Can Recycling Information Bureau)
- Recycling aluminium can bring energy savings of up to 95%, reduces import costs, and produces 95% less greenhouse gas emissions than when it is produced from raw materials.
  (Source: alupro)
- About 20,000 tonnes of aluminium foil packaging (worth £8 million) is wasted each year. Only 3,000 tonnes is recycled (worth £1.2 million).
  (Source: alupro)
- If all the aluminium cans sold in the UK were recycled, there would be 12 million fewer full dustbins each year.
  (Source: Alucan website)

Paper (e.g. newspapers and magazines)

- Each tonne of paper recycled saves 15 average-sized trees, as well as their surrounding habitat and wildlife.
  (Source: World Wildlife Fund)
- Reclaimed waste paper represents around 63% of the fibre used to produce paper and board in the UK.
  (Source: The Paper & Pulp Information Centre)

Glass (e.g. glass bottles and jars)

- Up to 90% of new glass can be made from reclaimed scrap glass, which saves energy and raw materials.
  (Source: British Glass)

Facts

- In just over a week, we produce enough rubbish to fill Wembley stadium. Over half can be recycled.
  (Source: DETR)
- The volume of waste produced in the UK in one hour would fill the Albert Hall.
  (Source: LGB Publications)
- In one day there would be enough waste to fill Trafalgar Square up to the top of Nelson's Column.
  (Source: LGB Publications)
- In one year there would be enough waste to fill dustbins stretching from the earth to the moon.
  (Source: LGB Publications)

- Glass packaging makes up about 9% by weight of the average household dustbin but accounts for over 70% by weight of packaging recycled from the total household waste stream.
  (Source: British Glass)
- In the UK, we use over 6 billion glass containers each year, equating to over 2 million tonnes. In 1998 we recycled 22% of these containers – the European average is 50%, with some countries recycling over 80%.
  (Source: British Glass)
- There are 22,000 bottle bank sites in the UK.
  (Source: British Glass)

Plastic (e.g. carrier bags and plastic bottles and pots)

- It is estimated that if 30% of the current consumption of thermoplastics in the UK could be recycled to replace virgin raw materials, substantial energy savings would be achieved and carbon dioxide emissions would be reduced by about 3 million tonnes/year.
  (Source: ETSU)
- Of the 2.4 million tonnes of plastic waste, an estimated 1,400,000 tonnes is household plastic waste, 200,000 tonnes is 'process scrap', and 800,000 tonnes is commercial waste. 61% of the total plastic waste from Western Europe is packaging, which typically has a 'life' of less than 12 months.
  (Source: AEA Technology)

Packaging generally

- Packaging is typically 25-35% by weight of dustbin waste, but developments in material strength and manufacturing technologies have allowed less material to contain the same volume of goods. Compared to 50 years ago:
  – food cans are 50% lighter;
  – yoghurt pots are 60% lighter;
  – glass milk bottles are 50% lighter;
  – plastic carrier bags are half as thick.
  Reducing the weight of packaging saves on transport costs and emissions as well as reducing consumption of raw materials.
  (Source: INCPEN)

Other household waste (e.g. kitchen food scraps, books and unwanted toys)

- Your waste can have a value to someone else – take old clothes, books, toys and bric-a-brac to charity shops or car boot sales.
  (Source: INCPEN)
- About a third of household waste is kitchen and garden waste – help reduce it by adding vegetable peelings and fruit skins to your compost heap.
  (Source: INCPEN)
- Another third of the dustbin is paper – ask your dentist or doctor if they would like old magazines for their waiting room and support paper recycling schemes.
  (Source: INCPEN)

- The above information is from the web site www.doingyourbit.org.uk

Waste

Information from Global Action Plan

The problem with rubbish is that we're throwing away so much more than we used to – including lots of things that aren't easily disposed of.

What's so bad about burying our rubbish?

90% of our rubbish goes to landfill sites – huge and sometimes leaky underground rubbish tips. Firstly, in the UK, we're running out of places to build landfill sites. As the waste decomposes, it produces two dangerous substances:

- Methane gas, which contributes to the greenhouse effect (causing climate change).
- Leachate, which can seep into our water supply, causing pollution.

So why not burn more of our rubbish?

Sending waste up into thin air sounds like the perfect solution for getting rid of it. But burning waste can release a range of pollutants into the atmosphere. The ash that is left over is often toxic and has to be disposed of in . . . yes, you've guessed it – landfill sites.

Is recycling the answer?

It's part of it, along with cutting down on the rubbish we create. Recycling also cuts down on raw materials having to be extracted from the earth's resources.

Did you know?

- In just over a week, we produce enough rubbish to fill (what was) Wembley stadium. Over half can be recycled.
  (DETR)
- In one year there would be enough waste to fill dustbins stretching from the earth to the moon.
  (LGB Publications)
- Every year in the UK we use 13 billion steel cans which, placed end to end, would stretch to the moon – three times!
  (Steel Can Recycling Information Bureau)
- If all the aluminium cans sold in the UK were recycled, there would be 12 million fewer full dustbins each year.
  (Alucan website)
- For every tonne of rubbish we throw away at home, another five tonnes were created when it was manufactured. And a further 20 tonnes were created when collecting the raw materials!
- In 1998 we recycled less than a quarter of glass containers – the European average is half, with some countries recycling over three-quarters.
  (British Glass)

Here's how you can reduce your waste . . .

- Don't leave litter on the street or in the playground.
- Encourage your school to set up recycling bins, if they haven't already.
- Suggest that your parents take a cloth shopping bag when they go shopping – then you won't be given lots of wasteful plastic bags.
- When drawing or writing, use both sides of paper.
- If you send a letter, reuse envelopes with reuse stickers.
- Sell unwanted stuff at a car boot sale, or donate it to a charity shop.
- If you can, have things repaired rather than throwing them away.
- Ask your parents if you can set up a wormery to recycle your organic waste.

■ The above information is from *Ergo* – the lifestyle magazine and consumer guide to sustainable living produced by Global Action Plan. See their web site at www.globalactionplan.org.uk or www.ergo-living.com

© *Global Action Plan*

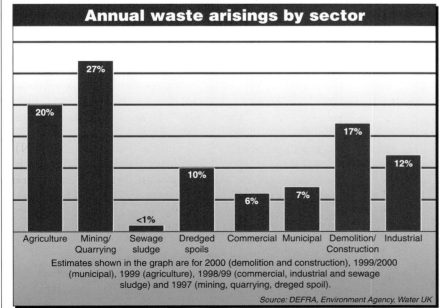

Annual waste arisings by sector

- Agriculture: 20%
- Mining/Quarrying: 27%
- Sewage sludge: <1%
- Dredged spoils: 10%
- Commercial: 6%
- Municipal: 7%
- Demolition/Construction: 17%
- Industrial: 12%

Estimates shown in the graph are for 2000 (demolition and construction), 1999/2000 (municipal), 1999 (agriculture), 1998/99 (commercial, industrial and sewage sludge) and 1997 (mining, quarrying, dreged spoil).

Source: DEFRA, Environment Agency, Water UK

The problem with incineration

Information from Greenpeace

Incinerators do not destroy waste. Every year in the UK, we produce millions of tonnes of domestic waste. We chuck it in the bin and wait for the council to collect it. Only 11% is recycled. The majority is landfilled or burnt, in 15 municipal incinerators around the country. Many people assume it has been destroyed.

But it is one of the fundamental principles of science that matter can never be destroyed; it can only ever be transformed. Incinerators do not destroy waste. They simply turn it into ash, gases and particulate matter. Our rubbish still exists. We may see less of it. But we're breathing it in instead.

Incinerators release a deadly cocktail of chemicals – from their chimney-stacks, in grate (bottom) ash and in water discharged to the sewerage system. The heat of the incinerator furnace vaporises some of the hazardous heavy metals – such as mercury, lead, cadmium, chromium and tin – found in household waste. And it causes chemical reactions, producing many new toxic chemicals, such as dioxins, polychlorinated biphenyls (PCBs), polychlorinated naphthalenes, chlorinated benzenes, polyaromatic hydrocarbons (PAHs). Other pollutants, such as sulphur dioxide and nitrogen oxides, are also released in huge quantities.

Incinerator emissions poison the human body. Cancer, heart disease, respiratory problems, immune system defects, increased allergies and birth defects can all be caused by the chemicals that spew out of large incinerators. Dioxins have been classified by the World Health Organisation (WHO) as carcinogenic, and have been described as the most toxic chemicals known to science. And yet more than half of British babies and toddlers exceed safe levels of dioxin intake.

Incinerator emissions are poorly regulated. Less than half of the chemicals they produce are continuously monitored. Independent dioxin monitoring occurs no more than twice a year, and the operators are warned in advance roughly when this will be done. A Belgian study has shown that dioxin levels, if continuously monitored, may be 30-50 times higher than the figure that emerges from this monitoring.

Incineration is not 'green'. New incinerators, such as the SELCHP plant in Lewisham, call themselves 'combined heat and power stations' and claim to produce 'green energy'. But generating energy from waste in this way is extremely polluting and inefficient. Burning materials that could be recycled and composted to recover a small fraction of the energy embodied in them is in no way green. Britain already has a massive

---

Incinerators do not destroy waste. They simply turn it into ash, gases and particulate matter. Our rubbish still exists. We may see less of it. But we're breathing it in instead

---

potential resource of green energy in wind, wave and solar power. And investing taxpayers' money in so-called 'energy from waste' schemes is to ignore these valuable and lucrative resources.

The government is reacting in blind panic. Pressure to comply with the EU Landfill Directive is forcing both central and local government to embrace incineration technology as a quick-fix solution – with little regard for impacts on health or the environment.

The UK can easily comply with the Landfill Directive without incineration – by recycling or composting just 30% of household newspaper, card and organic waste by 2010.

■ The above information is from Greenpeace's web site which can be found at www.greenpeace.org.uk

© Greenpeace

INCINERATION TURNS OUR WASTE INTO THIN AIR!

...DO I KEEP HOLDING MY BREATH?

Fridge mountain could cost £40m

By Paul Brown,
Environment Correspondent

The mountains of second-hand fridges that have been stacked up round Britain since January will cost the taxpayer £40m to deal with – an entirely unnecessary expense caused by government incompetence, according to the Commons environment, food and rural affairs select committee.

New rules by the European commission on the disposal of fridges which meant foam containing CFCs had to be stripped out to protect the ozone layer, were not understood or clarified by civil servants and ministers were kept in the dark about the consequences, the committee found.

The committee said the government's attempt to blame the fridge debacle on Eurocrats was wrong.

'While the EC must accept some blame for lack of clarity, the overwhelming responsibility for mishandling the implementation of the regulation lies with the government.'

British officials failed to understand the issue when other countries correctly implemented it immediately. They also failed to spot that the regulation stopped the industry exporting second-hand fridges to the developing world, adding significantly to the disused fridge mountain.

'They apparently ignored or reacted very slowly to a host of warnings from interested parties; and despite those warnings and legal advice suggesting that the regulation would be taken to apply to foam insulation, they failed to put in place contingency plans to cope with the problem.'

The committee is concerned that the same problem will happen again and says the problem is urgent because of regulations already accepted to deal with scrap cars, computers and mobile telephones.

Already the government is failing to act on a similar directive on used cars which should have been implemented in April. This is intended to avoid pollution from oil and other substances in scrap cars but so far the machinery to deal with it has not been installed. And it is not yet decided who will pay for the disposal of the waste.

The implications of another regulation on electrical goods due to come in next year are also not understood.

The committee wants a full review of how EU regulations are scrutinised for their implications, and complains of undue haste in adopting them.

The issue of who is to pay for fridge disposal has still not been resolved and the committee is asking for further information on what happens when the current mountain of one million fridges is dealt with. The mountain is growing at the rate of 40,000 a week.

Dumped on

First there were fridge mountains, now the government is faced with the prospect of figuring out what to do with Britain's millions of used tyres

By Mark Rowe

Whoever set fire to the huge Heyope tyre dump near Knighton, Powys, in 1989 could have had little idea that the action would enter the record books. Almost 13 years later, Britain's longest burning tyre fire smoulders gently on.

The tyres – all 10m of them – lie in a deep wooded valley in the Welsh borders. They are packed too densely for firefighters to extinguish and there are no flames, but temperature readings confirm the intense heat generated below the surface. Wisps of acrid black smoke occasionally drift up from the mass of rubber.

Scrap tyres are about to become the latest headache for a government still smarting from the debacle over its newly-created fridge mountain. A European directive will ban landfills of whole tyres by next year and shredded tyres by 2006. The option of dumping tyres in places like Heyope will be closed and new ways will have to be found to dispose of the 13m tyres that are stockpiled or put in landfills every year. The problem is huge. The number of tyres in use is forecast to increase by up to 60% by 2021, as the number of vehicles rises. Every day, 100,000 are taken off cars, vans, trucks, buses and bicycles. It is widely estimated that there are now more than 200m lying around.

'By their very nature, tyres are difficult to dispose of,' says David Santillo, from the Greenpeace research laboratories, based at Exeter University. 'They are designed not to fall apart while you're driving along the motorway, so they are one of the more intractable issues.'

Although tyres remain substantially intact for decades, some of their components can break down and leach. Environmental conern centres on the highly toxic additives used in their manufacture, such as zinc, chromium, lead, copper, cadmium and sulphur.

The environment agency is launching a campaign later this month to alert the public and industry to the need to prolong the life of existing tyres and find new recycling methods. 'You can find landfill sites that cover an entire valley, with black as far as the eye can see,' says an agency spokesman. 'We have always viewed tyres as a resource, rather than something to be dumped.'

The best use of tyres is probably to retread them, but this is now expensive, and fewer than ever are recycled in this way. According to the Used Tyre Working Group, a joint industry and government initiative sponsored by the main tyre industry associations, just 18% of Britain's tyres are retreaded. A further 48,500 tonnes are converted into 'crumb rubber', used in carpet underlay and to make surfaces such as those on running tracks and children's playgrounds.

More controversially, a further 18% are burnt as a 'replacement fuel' in the manufacture of cement. This is fast becoming the most popular way of disposing of them, but it is of increasing concern to environmentalists and scientists.

'Tyre burning emits ultra-fine particles that have a toxicity all of their own,' says Vyvyan Howard, senior lecturer in toxicopathology at Liverpool University. 'The toxicity is even stronger if this contains metals such as nickel and tin, which you get when you throw the whole tyre into the furnace. If the metal content of the particles goes up, then there is going to be an increasing impact on health.'

The cement companies deny that they are affecting people's health.

Meanwhile, the UK sends 26% of its tyres to landfill, far less than some other EU countries. France sends almost half, Spain 58%, but Holland sends none. The industry is now racking its brains as to how to dispose of the extra 13m tyres that will accumulate from the end of next year.

Santillo believes the onus is on the manufacturers to produce tyres that lend themselves to greater

recycling. 'Tyre burning is a very attractive short-term option, but it is disingenuous,' he says. 'In the medium term, we have to look at the options for recycling, but longer term we must look at the sort of hazardous materials that are going into tyres in the first place.'

Burning issues over old tyres

Blue Circle, Britain's largest cement maker, uses scrap tyres as a replacement fuel at its plant at Westbury, Wiltshire. The company argues that this is a 'win-win' situation for the environment: fewer fossil fuels are burned and the tyres are reused instead of being deposited in landfill sites; and Blue Circle benefits, since the 4m tyres it plans to burn every year help save the company an estimated £6m a year.

The company says that trials at the plant in 1999 showed that burning tyres reduces the company's impact on the local environment by 27% and decreases emissions of smog-causing oxides of nitrogen. Tyres burned at intense temperatures (1,450C to 2,000C), it says, produce no black smoke or acrid smell.

A local pressure group, The Air That We Breathe, disagrees. They say that tyre burning causes emissions of sulphur dioxide to rise tenfold and emissions of dust particles to increase 500%.

UK sends 26% of its tyres to landfill, far less than some other EU countries

---

They also claim that carcinogenic dioxins are produced by the burning of the chlorinated elements in the tyres – and they are now seeking leave for a judicial review of the decision to allow Blue Circle to burn tyres.

Underwater attraction?

One alternative reuse of tyres that has been tested around the world is tyre reefs. These are made up of old tyres bound together and dropped in the sea. It is widely hoped that they can become breeding grounds for fish and crustaceans.

Scientists at Southampton Oceanography Centre (SOC) put 500 tyres together to form a reef the size of a tennis court and dropped it into Poole Bay, Dorset, in 1998. The reef has thrived and now boasts species such as lobsters and wrasse.

'The marine life growing on the reef is not affected by the substances that come out of the tyre,' says Ken Collins, senior research fellow at the SOC. 'The growth of life on the tyres is as prolific as on an ordinary reef.'

The findings may suggest a potential use for scrap tyres in coastal defences around the UK and elsewhere.

'Are tyres under water harmless? No, but they are not very harmful,' says Collins. 'Tyres in the sea are extremely stable. Not a lot comes out of them. Most pollution in the sea caused by tyres comes from the pollutants that come off working tyres and are washed from the road into the sea by rainwater.'

© *Guardian Newspapers Limited 2002*

Litter

The big picture

Did you know . . . ?

- An aluminium can takes up to 100 years to break down naturally.
- Local councils spend about £332 million every year cleaning litter from streets in Britain.
- In a recent survey, 90% of people questioned said they were concerned about littered pavements.

What is litter? And in what way is it different from waste minimisation? Of course, litter is very closely linked to waste. The best way to explain the difference is to say that litter is waste in the wrong place, such as on the pavement or the school field rather than in the bin. Like graffiti or vandalism, litter has a strong effect on the impression people have of an area's quality.

Litter has many forms and many sources. It can be anything from a dropped sweet wrapper or the spilled contents of a car ashtray to a fly-tipped load of demolition rubble. Unlike some other forms of pollution, it can be difficult to identify exactly who is responsible. Because it is often impossible to punish offenders directly, raising general awareness of the issue becomes even more important.

Making a mess

Litter is always caused by people. Although you could say that nature causes its own litter, for example,

dead leaves and twigs from trees, the difference is that this natural waste is usually fully biodegradable. It rots away quickly, enriching the soil and supporting the growth of new vegetation as it does so. Human litter takes a long time to degrade naturally, and can sometimes hang around indefinitely, ruining the appearance of towns and countryside.

Litter and the law

The Environmental Protection Act, introduced in 1990, made littering a crime subject to a maximum fine of £2,500. Local councils are responsible for keeping their streets clean and can be prosecuted for failing to do so.

The Act sets out standards of cleanliness for public places. These standards combine a visual assessment of the amount of litter with fixed deadlines for cleaning up. This approach has changed the way councils operate. Instead of regular rounds, many councils now use a more flexible approach so they can respond quickly to unexpected problems.

Dangerous litter

Litter doesn't just spoil how things look; it can also be a health hazard. Food litter can attract rats and flies, which spread disease. Dog fouling in public areas (another form of litter) is a serious health risk.

Litter can also be lethal to wildlife. For example, drinks left in discarded bottles often attract small animals like mice, which can squeeze into the bottles but may drown or be unable to climb the smooth, sloping surface to get out. Discarded fishing lines can maim and kill water birds. Plastic bags can look like food to cows, sheep, horses and marine life, but can kill if swallowed.

Litter and waste

Cleaning up litter is an important step, but simply putting rubbish in the bin is not the end of the story.

Litter has many forms and many sources. It can be anything from a dropped sweet wrapper or the spilled contents of a car ashtray to a fly-tipped load of demolition rubble

- Eco Schools was originated and is coordinated internationally by the Foundation for Environmental Education.

Eco Schools is managed by Encams. Encams is a campaigning charity working to create a better environment. It is recognised as the national agency for litter abatement and manages the Eco Schools programme in the UK.

- The above information is from the web site www.eco-schools.org.uk

© Eco Schools

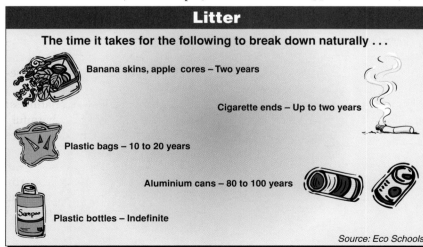

Litter

The time it takes for the following to break down naturally . . .

Banana skins, apple cores – Two years

Cigarette ends – Up to two years

Plastic bags – 10 to 20 years

Aluminium cans – 80 to 100 years

Plastic bottles – Indefinite

Source: Eco Schools

The litter issue

Information from The Industry Council for Packaging and the Environment (INCPEN)

INCPEN actively supports initiatives to tackle the problem of litter and works closely with ENCAMS (formerly the Tidy Britain Group). It has published its own surveys on public attitudes to litter and on local authorities' expenditure on litter clearance.

Litter is any waste in the wrong place. It can be a drinks can, a fast-food box, a cigarette pack, a newspaper or an old tyre and it may be unhealthy or dangerous like broken glass or a banana skin.

The ultimate solution is to change public attitudes once and for all, so that deliberate littering becomes socially unacceptable and thoughtless littering less common. There are signs that this process is well under way, with the public becoming more aware that a litter-free environment is an achievable aim. ENCAM's campaign reinforces the need for public co-operation and its publicity, education programmes and major events reach people at all levels.

Whilst public co-operation is vital, so too is the part that statutory organisations play. Part IV of the Environmental Protection Act 1990, dealing with litter, marked a major change in the enforcement of anti-litter measures. The Act's accompanying Code of Practice on Litter and Refuse sets new standards for street cleanliness. In particular, local authorities are required to cleanse streets and town centres, both routinely and whenever needed. Litter bins provided by the local authority now feature in our high streets.

The causes of litter

Litter often results from careless or inconsiderate actions by pedestrians or motorists but can also be created by mishandled domestic waste, industrial refuse, loading or unloading of vehicles, construction sites or vehicles travelling with uncovered or insecure loads. Sources of litter may not always be identifiable as it does not necessarily stay where it is dropped. Waste can be blown by the wind until it reaches an obstacle, creating a litter trap.

Packaging and litter

Attempts to solve the problem by singling out particular products or packs invariably fail because they don't take account of human behaviour and changes in lifestyle. For instance, people are consuming more food and drink outdoors and smoking is prohibited on some public transport and in many areas. Some American states have tried to curb litter by placing mandatory deposits on beverage containers but these have not helped reduce the overall amount of litter. Community-based litter abatement programmes, similar to those of the ENCAMS, have proved much more successful.

Packaging manufacturers and users are concerned about litter and play an active part – both individually and through INCPEN – in anti-litter projects, educational programmes and research. Designers are taking account of where packaging might be discarded by adding litter prevention slogans or using non-detachable ring pulls on cans. Plastic ring carriers for cans are now photodegradable so they break up in sunlight.

What can be done

People create litter: only people can cure it!

Research shows that people care less about adding to existing litter than being the first offender. It follows that streets kept clean and litter-free are more likely to remain that way.

To tackle litter effectively, several measures need to be taken:

- Opportunities must be taken to emphasise to the public that the offence of littering is unacceptable and unnecessary.
- Local authorities should organise efficient and prompt collection of domestic and trade refuse so that it is not left to obstruct the pavement or get scattered.

- Streets and other public places must be kept clear of litter to comply with the cleanliness standards contained in the Code of Practice on Litter and Refuse. The cleanliness standards specify the times allowed to bring an area to Grade A i.e. litter-free. This new approach embodies the principle 'If it's not dirty – don't clean it' so that resources can be concentrated where they are most needed.
- The Tidy Britain Group's People and Places Programme is a long-term strategy designed to help local authorities meet their responsibilities under the Code of Practice on Litter and Refuse
- Local authorities and citizens alike should make full use of the new powers contained in Part IV of the Environmental Protection Act 1990 to combat litter:

A local authority can be held legally responsible if an area under its control is not kept clean. The maximum fine for the offence of littering is £2,500. Local authorities can appoint a litter warden empowered to impose a £10 fixed

penalty fine on litterers. Local authorities can also issue Street Litter Control Notices or designate Litter Control Areas to ensure that owners are responsible for keeping their 'patch' clean. They also have the power to collect and charge for abandoned shopping trolleys.

'Accounting for litter'

The aim of this survey into litter accounting practices, carried out by Ernst & Young on behalf of INCPEN, was to assist local authorities to direct their scarce resources to where they would have most effect by measuring their performance against national statistics.

Over 200 local authorities participated in the survey. The research showed that there was no consistency in the way authorities accounted for litter abatement services so it was difficult to monitor the cost effectiveness of such services. However, it did show that the vast majority of litter abatement expenditure was on 'cure' such as street cleaning and only a small proportion was spent on preventative methods. The report recommended an accounting framework for prevention and cure activities which could improve the quality of litter accounting information in local authorities and contribute to the development of a national picture for comparison on the most cost effective forms of litter abatement.

- INCPEN is currently reviewing the situation with local authorities particularly now that the new legislative requirements under the Environmental Protection Act have to be met.

- The above information is from INCPEN's web site which can be found at www.incpen.org
© The Industry Council for Packaging and the Environment (INCPEN)

Time to cut back on the rat pack

Scared of rats? Stop reading now

Human beings have an aversion to rats. It could stem from medieval times and the Black Death which wiped out a third of the UK population (although it was the fleas that black rats harboured rather than the rodents themselves that spread the killer disease). It might also be as simple as their often-demonised appearance – bloodshot eyes, wiry tail – or the infections they are known to carry, that make them so unappealing. Whatever the reason, to many of us, rats are the stuff of nightmares.

What a pity then that human beings don't have those same feelings of revulsion for the one single factor that has helped expand the rat

By Peter Gibson, Media Manager, ENCAMS

population to an estimated 60 million. Namely, food litter.

The figures speak for themselves. According to the pest control industry, the amount of rodent infestations has grown by 24 per cent over the last two years – including big rises in the South East of England and West Midlands. Consider this statistic too, estimates put the amount of rubbish dropped per year in 1964 at five million tonnes. By 2001, that figure was above 25 million tonnes. Could it be

any coincidence that the first fast food restaurant opened in 1964? Put simply, Britain's obsession with food on the go has resulted in a growing litter problem and a massive rise in vermin.

But our throwaway habits haven't only helped swell the number

According to the pest control industry, the amount of rodent infestations has grown by 24 per cent over the last two years

of rats – they've also changed their behaviour. We now have a generation of rodents entirely dependent on human beings for their diet and with no incentive to return to the shadows or the sewers; these rats are now moving into our space. And that means our homes, businesses, buildings and as recent television footage showed, even into the parks where our children play. The success of bait also depends on rats returning to the place where they first found their food source and with a huge feast to choose from, rodents are becoming increasingly immune. Picking up the tab for this problem are local authorities and such is the strain of responding to complaints that 16 per cent of them (mostly in affluent areas) are now charging up to £65 for rat removal.

The one plus point about the connection between rats and fast food litter, is that by preying upon this human fear of rodents, we can actually solve the rubbish problem. Under its Keep Britain Tidy banner, ENCAMS has unveiled a campaign called: 'How Close Do You Want Them To Get?' which (as the title suggests) aims to hammer home the message that by dropping sandwiches, burgers, crisps and pizzas the public are bringing rats into the human zone. Its main thrust is a cinema advert which is currently running before the Hollywood blockbuster *Men in Black II* (deliberately chosen as it appeals to Britain's worst litter louts, young men). The advert has been described by critics as a 'spine tingling chiller'

and aside from images of rats scurrying about amongst burger cartons and fish and chip papers, it climaxes on the shot of a couple in a bed full of rats. This shocking scene was recreated at the advert's premiere in early August 2002 and captured not only the interest of the national media here in Britain but has also been broadcast as far afield as Germany, South Africa and the US.

The advert is also being shown at screens in bars at Premiership and leading first division football clubs and posters featuring the strap-line, 'The more food you drop, the closer we get' will be appearing at 8,000 sites across Britain.

We now have a generation of rodents entirely dependent on human beings for their diet and with no incentive to return to the shadows or the sewers

---

In partnership with the Government, ENCAMS is also setting up a Fast Food Code of Practice. At present there is no single body that represents the industry, so swapping good practice on any issue is problematic. The express aim of the code is to get the industry to adhere to a set of principles that will ensure all owners – whether they manage a large chain or just a hot-dog stand – keep a tidy shop. Environment Minister Michael

Meacher has also signalled his intent to crack down on illegal vendors who often fail to provide bins for their customers.

The response to the campaign so far has been warm and aside from the media putting the issue of litter back on the agenda (and getting their phone lines jammed by the irate British public), initial feedback to the cinema advert has revealed that respondents among the core group of litterers – teenage boys – have promised to ditch their dirty habits. Time will tell, of course, but if we don't want our streets to be overrun by rodents we need to ensure that the fast food generation does us all a favour – and takes away this problem by using a bin.

■ The above article first appeared in *Wastes Management*, September 2002, produced by the Chartered Institution of Wastes Management. See page 41 for their address details.
© *The Chartered Institution of Wastes Management*

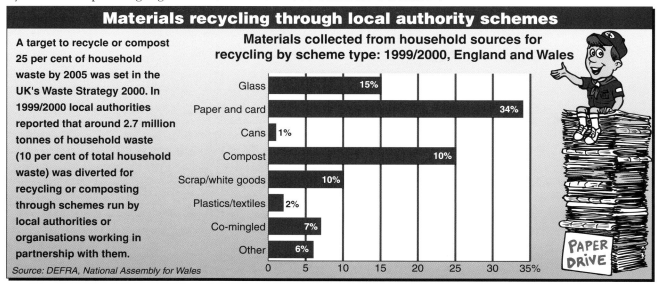

Materials recycling through local authority schemes

A target to recycle or compost 25 per cent of household waste by 2005 was set in the UK's Waste Strategy 2000. In 1999/2000 local authorities reported that around 2.7 million tonnes of household waste (10 per cent of total household waste) was diverted for recycling or composting through schemes run by local authorities or organisations working in partnership with them.

Source: DEFRA, National Assembly for Wales

Materials collected from household sources for recycling by scheme type: 1999/2000, England and Wales

Material	Percentage
Glass	15%
Paper and card	34%
Cans	1%
Compost	10%
Scrap/white goods	10%
Plastics/textiles	2%
Co-mingled	7%
Other	6%

Marine litter

Information from the Marine Conservation Society

Background

Marine litter is the collective term for any man-made object present in the marine environment.

Litter can be attributed to four main source groups:

- Recreational and tourism-related litter
- Sewage-related debris
- Fishing debris
- Shipping waste

The relative proportions of these four main sources may differ considerably between regions – some beaches may be more affected by shipping and fishing debris than by tourist litter depending on the scale of local activities.

In the majority of Beachwatch beach litter surveys over 50% of the litter recorded is made from plastic, echoing the wide-ranging uses to which plastics are put. Items include: cotton buds, bottles, sheeting, nets, multi-pack drink can yokes, sweet wrappers . . . the list is endless.

Impacts

There are two main dangers to wildlife from litter at sea:

Entanglement

- Animals may become entangled in discarded or lost nets, strapping bands, drink can yokes and ropes, which can cause flesh wounds, strangulation and drowning. Fishing nets, fishing line, plastic strapping and can carriers are the most common cause of entanglement, they reduce movement and can result in serious injury and death by starvation, drowning or suffocation.

- Studies show that approximately 30,000 northern fur seals die annually due to entanglement, primarily in net fragments.
- Plastics are also used as nesting material. Over 90% of the 30,000 gannet nests on Grassholm Island now contain plastic. Young gannets' feet can often become entangled, resulting in serious injuries.

Ingestion

- Marine animals also mistake plastic items for food, which if ingested can cause starvation and poisoning. Whole plastic bags and gallon drums can be mistakenly identified as food and eaten by some mammal, turtle and shark species. These items can physically block the intestinal tract, causing starvation and internal injuries as well as containing toxic chemicals.
- Globally, an estimated one million birds and 100,000 marine mammals and sea turtles die every year from entanglement in, or ingestion, of plastics.
- Of the 115 species of marine mammals, 47 are known to become entangled in and/or ingest marine debris.

Impacts on man

- Broken glass and discarded medical equipment may cause injury to beach visitors.
- Coastal resorts which rely on tourism can suffer substantial economic loss if washed-up plastic and sewage-related debris destroys the appeal of its beaches or rocky shores.
- Marine litter may also result in lost revenue for fisheries, due to the time and effort involved in sorting debris from the catch, while larger items may actually tear the fishing gear.

You can help stop the pollution of the seas from litter and plastic debris in the following ways:

What you can do

- Join in with national initiatives like MCS Beachwatch to clean beaches and gather information on the levels and sources of UK coastal litter. Adopt-a-Beach and become part of the UK's largest national initiative to combat the problems of coastal litter – contact MCS.
- Reduce the amount of plastic you use. Use fabric shopping bags instead of plastic carriers. Avoid buying pre-packed goods or those that have an unnecessary amount of packaging.
- Reuse plastic containers wherever possible.
- Recycle plastic bottles if facilities are available, if not contact your local authority and urge them to expand their recycling capabilities.
- Make it safe: Cut any plastic rings or strapping before disposal.
- 'Bag it and bin it': Please don't flush plastic sanitary items and cotton buds down the toilet. Contact Bag it & Bin it campaign for more details.
- Follow the Seashore Code: Do not leave or bury any litter on beaches or allow litter to get into rivers. Contact MCS for copies of the *Seashore Code*. Take only memories – Leave nothing but footprints.
- Keep your litter on board: Find out what litter reception facilities are available at local ports and marinas. Contact the Maritime and Coastguard Agency.
- The above information is from the Marine Conservation Society's web site which can be found at www.mcsuk.org

© *Marine Conservation Society*

EU drive on recycling 'too fast' for Britain

By Ian Black in Brussels

British manufacturers came under new pressure to recycle up to 65% of all packaging after a vote in the European parliament yesterday.

Under the plan, to be implemented by 2006, 1994 rules designed to limit environmental damage are to be extended and updated to tackle mounting levels of domestic waste.

It could also mean local councils will have to spend more to collect rubbish separated into different recycling categories.

Britain, which lags behind most other EU members in recycling and is still struggling with 'fridge mountains' created by separate rules agreed in Brussels, had wanted the measures delayed until 2008.

The proposals include concrete targets to reduce packaging waste – glass, paper, cardboard, metals and plastics – used to wrap goods from chocolate bars and tea bags to flower pots.

Euro MPs voted by 487 to six to back the plan, which will be sent to all EU governments for consultation and then back to the parliament for a final vote.

Manufacturers, who have been lobbying against the scheme, will be held responsible for reducing packaging. Existing EU legislation already requires producers to cover the costs of recycling 45% of their packaging. By 2004, new packaging can only be put on the market if manufacturers have taken 'all necessary measures to minimise its environmental impact'.

British Labour MEPs welcomed the vote but warned against trying to do too much too fast. 'We are drowning in a sea of milk cartons, hairspray and Coke cans and awash with pizza boxes and wine bottles,' said David Bowe, Labour's environment spokesman.

> ## 'We all want to see a reduction in the amount of packaging waste, but laws need to be realistic'

'If this legislation signals the end of one more elaborate box around a fancy bottle, wrapped in plastic and sold with a carton in a heavyweight bag, it will have done its job.

'With landfills reaching capacity and incinerators at overflow, the wads of packaging we use have got to go.'

The proposals are seen as part of a wider culture change for business and consumers alike to limit the damage the 'disposable society' does to the environment.

John Bowis, the Conservative spokesman, said too much haste would be counterproductive and would endanger the stability of the UK's waste management sector, while imposing vast additional costs on industry.

'We all want to see a reduction in the amount of packaging waste, but laws need to be realistic,' he said. 'Member states and European industry are seriously unprepared for a target date of 2006. While we accept that the UK needs to catch up with much of Europe, present increased efforts could be ruined by pushing too far, too fast.'

EU countries have widely different recycling rates. Germany, Sweden and Austria lead the pack in efficiency, while Ireland and Greece languish at the bottom of the table.

Eluned Morgan, Labour MEP, said: 'Business has taken on a lot of the responsibility until now. By setting this target slightly higher again, it means for the first time that local authorities will have to get more involved. People will have to start separating their rubbish.'

Rubbish! That's our recycling record

For 10 short days, representatives and heads of state from at least 174 countries descended upon Johannesburg for the earth summit – the UN's world conference on sustainable development. It was the biggest convention ever orchestrated by the UN. On the agenda were poverty and development, increasing access to safe water, global warming, and how far the world's nations have come to meeting the environmental promises they made at the earth summit in Rio de Janeiro 10 years ago. By Laura Barton

Britain has not come far enough. John Prescott, the deputy prime minister, claims that Britain has been at the very fore in promoting global environmental issues, casting off its image as 'the dirty man of Europe'. But although the government has increased the aid budget dramatically, and has promoted the integration of trade, development and environmental issues, Britain still has a very long way to go.

Each year, Britain throws away 435 million tonnes of rubbish, of which 106 million tonnes is household waste. The majority goes into landfill sites. There are 1,400 such sites in the UK, though the country is under increasing pressure from the EU to reduce this figure. Waste is delivered to the landfill site, compressed and then buried. Grass is then planted over the top.

The dangers of landfill are manifold: they release toxic gases such as methane, carbon dioxide, hydrogen sulphide and vinyl chloride into the air, old batteries buried deep within the sites leak poisonous metals into the ground water. In recent years there have also been possible links to incidences of cancer. The alternative is burning the waste in an incinerator, which, although it occupies less space, is more expensive and also releases a bevy of noxious gases and leaves carcinogenic ash.

Britain urgently needs to find alternative ways of dealing with its rubbish. EU legislation states that two-thirds of waste must be sent anywhere but landfill by 2020, or else the country will face fines of up to £500,000 a day. Household waste alone is growing by 3% each year. Meanwhile just 12% of British household waste is recycled, a proportion that is increasing by a paltry 1% annually.

Britain is lagging far behind its European cousins. Germany, Switzerland and the Netherlands already recycle 50% of their waste. Proposals to shift Britain's attitude to waste disposal include charging people proportionately to the amount of rubbish they generate, and more rigorously enforcing recycling schemes. The plans reply upon re-educating the public. Few people realise how much rubbish they generate, or that much of it could be recycled. Who knew, for example, that each week, wealthier households chuck out approximately 5kg more waste than poorer ones, or that 35% of the weight and 50% of the volume of household rubbish is made up of packaging?

Plans are also afoot to introduce an environmental tax on plastic bags. Such a scheme was introduced in Ireland in March, and has already proved phenomenally successful. The 10p tax on supermarket carrier bags has meant that 90% fewer plastic bags have been provided, reducing use of non-recyclable bags by a billion and earning £2.25m. The Irish government intends to spend this on environmental programmes. Previously, approximately 1.2 billion free plastic bags were doled out every year. Martin Cullen, the Irish environmental minister, is naturally pleased: 'We are realising that by implementing practical measures such as this, the environment wins.'

Whatever the outcome of the Johannesburg conference, whatever treaties are signed, or pledges made, the truth is that improving the environment needn't involve millions of pounds, and hundreds of world leaders in suits. Saving the world can start in your own backyard.

Government must tackle waste crisis

Information from Friends of the Earth

Friends of the Earth

The Government's Strategy Unit today published an interim discussion document on the need to tackle the UK's mounting waste crisis (www.piu.gov.uk).

Friends of the Earth is calling on the Government to:

- Rule out the building of new mass-burn incinerators;
- Increase the UK domestic waste recycling target to at least 50 per cent by 2010;
- Ensure that every household has access to a doorstep recycling collection scheme;
- Put in place a comprehensive strategy to reduce waste.

Mike Childs, Waste campaigner at Friends of the Earth, said: 'The time has come for the Government to take decisive action to tackle the UK's growing waste crisis. Landfilling waste or burning it in incinerators is bad for the environment and deeply unpopular with the public. The UK must introduce doorstep recycling for every household and set a target of recycling at least half of our household waste by 2010. If our neighbours in Europe can achieve this, why can't we?'

Waste facts and figures

- The UK currently languishes near the bottom of the European recycling league table. Only around 11% of the UK's 28 million tonnes of domestic waste produced annually is recycled. This compares badly with neighbours such as Switzerland (52%), Austria (49.7%), Germany (48%) and the Netherlands (46%).
- The current government recycling target is a very unambitious 30 per cent by 2010. FOE says it should be at least 50 per cent by 2010.
- Nine out of ten people in England and Wales would recycle more waste if it was made easier, an Environment Agency survey revealed in May this year (EA Press Release 23 May 2002).
- In April the Environment Agency warned that space for burying rubbish in the South East could run out within seven years. Northern Ireland is already exporting some of its household waste to Scotland for landfill.
- Growing waste, unambitious recycling targets and rapidly filling landfill sites are leading more waste authorities to push for waste incineration. Many community groups around the country are opposing incineration proposals because of concerns about the risk to health and the environmental impact. Once built, incinerators need more and more waste, which could otherwise be recycled, to make them economically viable.
- Friends of the Earth is campaigning for a new law for mandatory doorstep recycling and composting service. A Parliamentary Motion supporting a doorstep scheme for every household (EDM 186) has already been signed by more than 200 MPs. It also has official support from both the Liberal Democrat and Conservative parties. If the Government fails to act, FOE will work with MPs that wish to introduce a new recycling law as a Private Member's Bill later this year.
- Around 80% of household waste could be either recycled or composted, dramatically reducing the need for landfill
- The above information is from Friends of the Earth's web site which can be found at www.foe.co.uk

© Friends of the Earth

Waste arisings and management

It is estimated that between 170 and 210 million tonnes of waste are produced each year in the UK, by households, commerce and industry, including construction and demolition. Nearly 60 per cent of this waste is disposed of to landfill sites. Around 55 per cent of industrial waste and commercial waste and 82 per cent of municipal waste is sent to landfill.

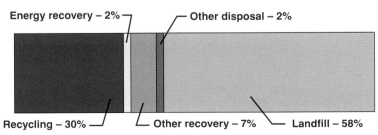

Energy recovery – 2% Other disposal – 2%
Recycling – 30% Other recovery – 7% Landfill – 58%

To comply with the Landfill Directive the Government has set targets to recover value from 40 per cent of municipal waste by 2005. The UK is also committed to reducing, by 2005, the amount of industrial and commercial waste sent to landfill to 85 per cent of that landfilled in 1997/98.

Source: DEFRA and others

Britain's abysmal record

Dismal recycling record leaves Britain with a rubbish reputation in the world of waste. Ministers race to end reliance on landfill and avoid stiff EU penalties

By Paul Brown and David Hencke

Britain's abysmal record of reuse and recycling of household waste, its mountain of disused fridges, and the widespread public resistance to plans to build incineration plants has sounded the alarm in Downing Street over the country's growing waste problem.

Cabinet Office proposals, revealed in the *Guardian* yesterday, to focus householders' minds on the problem by charging up to £1 a bag for rubbish not sorted for recycling could prove a political hot potato.

So far, householders have not been blamed for low levels of recycling. Environment agency surveys have shown that nine out of 10 people would recycle more waste if it were easier, but for many there were few facilities, and for some items such as plastic, no opportunity to do so at all.

Local authorities have been blamed for not giving the issue priority, although they argue that there is often no market for the recycled material they collect.

The proposal to charge householders was welcomed by environmentalists and the waste collecting and disposal industry.

Dirk Hazell, chief executive of the waste industry's trade body, the Environmental Services Association, said the cost of disposing of household waste – currently 50p a person a week – needed to be raised to £1 a week. He said those who threw the waste away, the householders, should pay for it.

But the Tory leader, Iain Duncan Smith, and the Liberal Democrats said the recommendations amounted to asking 'the public to pay twice' for the same services.

Mr Duncan Smith said: 'Millions of families are being asked to pay twice over for health, education, transport, rubbish collection and the post. We shouldn't have to pay twice just because the government haven't a clue how to reform public services. We deserve a lot better.'

Lady Miller of Chilthorne Domer, Liberal Democrat environment spokesman in the House of Lords and a county councillor in Somerset, said: 'This is a double tax because people are paying council tax.

> ## Britain's record of 11% recycled household waste is a quarter of its northern European neighbours

'In Somerset we have drawn up a waste management plan for kerbside recycling and we have had £1.1m from the government to help with the start-up. People are already paying their council tax and the government grant is already taxpayers' money. So why should they then pay again for their rubbish?'

Downing Street's official spokesman, meanwhile, emphasised that the idea still had to be accepted by the prime minister.

Britain's record of 11% recycled household waste is a quarter of its northern European neighbours. By 2016 EU law will force Britain to cut the 80% of its waste going to landfill down to 33%.

History helps to explain the disparity. While other countries were running out of holes to dump rubbish in the 1980s, Britain had plenty of former mines and quarries to use as landfill and ignored the impending EU legislation forcing a greater emphasis on reuse, recycling and composting.

But with household waste volume standing at 28m tonnes a year, and rising 3% annually, Britain suddenly found it had little hope of reaching the EU's legally binding targets of cutting landfill. EU rules state that half the rubbish that went into landfill in 1995 should, by 2009, be reused, composted or recycled. This target rises to 65% by 2016.

Britain faces prosecution in the European court and fines of millions of pounds a day if it fails to reach its targets.

The first reaction of the former department of environment to the looming landfill restrictions was to encourage a new generation of incinerators that would cut the volume of waste going into landfill by 80% and also produce electricity. It was estimated that up to 100 incinerators would be needed along with the 10 already in operation. Fierce opposition to every proposal, many of them in Labour seats, forced a u-turn.

WHAT'S THE ALTERNATIVE TO LANDFILL?

...AIRFILL...

There have been other hiccups. The obvious way to cut large volumes of waste is through garden compost, and large-scale municipal composting schemes. The current level of waste composted (2%) should rise to at least 20% and it could rise to 40% given large-scale projects. But the projects have been delayed due to the failure of the environment agency and health and safety executive to agree on whether it is safe or not to compost.

Possible health hazards of composting cooked kitchen waste mean many schemes have been outlawed. The National Trust, for example, was told to apply for a licence for every compost heap in its hundreds of gardens.

It also has proved impossible to agree on standards for compost content, prompting the scrapping or suspension of many promising schemes because the compost itself might be reclassified as waste because it contains ground glass or metal.

On the positive side, the Department of Environment, Food and Rural Affairs realised 18 months ago that the principal problem of reform was the lack of markets for both recycled material and compost. Newsprint offers the best example: old newspapers and magazines are both easy to collect and sort. One-third is recycled but prices for such old newsprint are low because there is not sufficient capacity in British mills to recycle it. Much is being exported and then recycled abroad.

The Waste and Resources Action Programme (Wrap),

established 18 months ago, provided funds to increase Britain's capacity, and deal with 320,000 extra tonnes a year at the Shotton mill in north Wales. As a result, newsprint recycling will rise from around one-third to about a half and there is room for a further mill. By 2004 all three British mills will be producing 100% recycled newsprint.

Wrap is spending £40m over three years developing other markets. Ground glass has enormous potential as a water filter to replace mined sand, and an experiment is taking place to use ground glass as a blasting medium to remove graffiti from stone and metalwork. Wrap plans to recycle an extra 300,000 tonnes of glass and 40,000 tonnes of plastic.

The environment minister, Michael Meacher, who was reportedly against charging householders to dispose of rubbish, said yesterday he had not ruled it out.

'Charging people would provide a useful extra incentive to reduce and recycle waste,' he said. 'The important thing first is to make sure that everyone has the facilities to compost and recycle. Already they can take unwanted items to the civic amenity tip but they need facilities at the kerbside and we want every council to do that.'

Mr Meacher has already trebled the recycling targets for 2005 and given local authorities an extra £140m to improve standards. 'I am determined to reach the targets,' he said.

© Guardian Newspapers Limited 2002

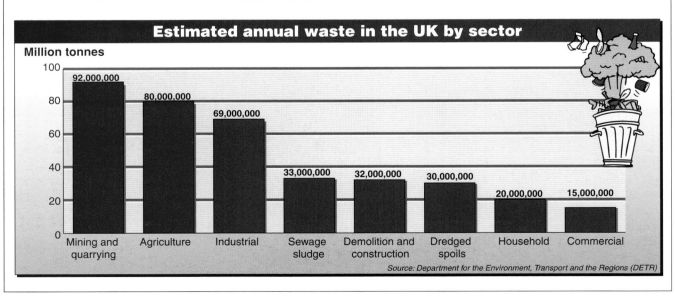

Estimated annual waste in the UK by sector

Million tonnes

- Mining and quarrying: 92,000,000
- Agriculture: 80,000,000
- Industrial: 69,000,000
- Sewage sludge: 33,000,000
- Demolition and construction: 32,000,000
- Dredged spoils: 30,000,000
- Household: 20,000,000
- Commercial: 15,000,000

Source: Department for the Environment, Transport and the Regions (DETR)

Waste minimisation

The big picture

In 1998, Britain generated 5 million tonnes of waste – enough to fill Wembley stadium about 50 times over. This is more than three times the amount we produced in 1986.

Disposing of this waste is difficult and costly. Most of it ends up in mountains of buried refuse called landfills. Even when managed properly, landfills can harm the local environment, poisoning the ground, atmosphere and any nearby water.

What are the alternatives to throwing away rubbish? Incineration is one space-saving solution, but has the drawback of releasing harmful emissions in to the air. Increasingly, the government is encouraging people to reduce the amount of rubbish they produce in the first place – by changing the way we buy products, by reusing products that can be reused and, where possible, by recycling.

Reduce, reuse, recycle

There are two main ways to reduce waste:

1. **Waste minimisation**: any measure taken before a product is purchased and used that reduces the quantity of waste the product will eventually create.
2. **Waste recovery**: material or energy recovery from reuse or recycling. This happens after a product is purchased and used.

To contribute to minimising the waste we produce, government and environmental researchers advise that, wherever it is practical and beneficial, people should take the following steps.

- Reduce waste – changing manufacturing processes so that less material is used, or changing buying habits so that less future waste material is bought.
- Reuse – choose goods and products that can be used again.

The government is encouraging people to reduce the amount of rubbish they produce in the first place

---

- Recycle – making sure that waste is processed and made into another product wherever possible. Composting is also recycling: the nutrients in organic waste are processed and returned to the soil to help more plants to grow.

Industry and consumers

Increasingly, the manufacturing industry is doing its bit to tackle the waste problem by reducing the amount of material used for packaging (this also helps to cut down on production costs). However, the total amount of waste produced by packaging is continuing to rise as we, the consumers, buy more products. We are going to have to make smarter choices in the way we buy products and reduce the amount we consume to reap the benefits of industry's reduction in the use of packaging materials.

Energy from waste

Energy from Waste (EfW) plants generate electricity from certain types of waste product by burning them. They provide an important alternative to recycling because, although all packaging can be recycled, it would not be environmentally efficient in terms of energy or materials for certain types of packaging to be collected and processed. Recovering energy from waste also helps to conserve fossil fuel sources as well as saving landfill

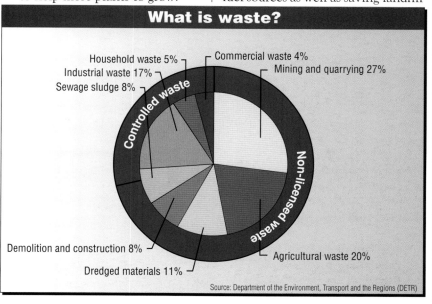

What is waste?

- Household waste 5%
- Industrial waste 17%
- Sewage sludge 8%
- Commercial waste 4%
- Mining and quarrying 27%
- Controlled waste
- Non-licensed waste
- Demolition and construction 8%
- Dredged materials 11%
- Agricultural waste 20%

Source: Department of the Environment, Transport and the Regions (DETR)

space for materials that cannot be disposed of through other means, such as demolition waste.

Markets for waste

One important way of reducing the amount of waste going to landfill is to find markets for waste – buyers for whom some of the materials that make up waste are actually valuable commodities.

Collection of waste materials must be in balance with market demand. Market demand varies depending on a number of factors, including the type of material available, its condition and geographical location. While clean, uncontaminated material can usually be sold to a reprocessor, lower-grade material can only be sold when there is a strong market demand.

To maintain the balance of supply and demand, nationwide systems of waste management need to be flexible. The system should allow for the extraction of recyclable material when demand is high and enable quick and efficient treatment and landfilling when demand is low.

What's the government doing?

Britain strengthened its waste strategy in May 2000. The government aims to redirect MSW treatment according to a timetable of targets:

- by 2005 – 25% recycled and composted, 15% to an EfW plant
- by 2010 – 30% recycled or composted, 15% to an EfW plant
- by 2015 – 33% recycled or composted, 33% to an EfW plant

The government's new strategy also includes help to develop markets for recycled materials. In October 2000, Prime Minister Blair announced that the UK government will invest over £50 million over three years in local arrangements for maximising recycling and composting. To boost public involvement in cutting waste, this funding will help provide kerbside recycling for 700,000 households.

- Eco Schools was originated and is coordinated internationally by the Foundation for Environmental Education.

Eco Schools is managed by Encams. Encams is a campaigning charity working to create a better environment. It is recognised as the national agency for litter abatement and manages the Eco Schools programme in the UK.

- The above information is from the web site www.eco-schools.org.uk

© Eco Schools

Top 20 waste tips

Information from Waste Watch

Once your rubbish is collected, most of it is buried in large holes in the ground. This is called landfilling. Some is burnt (incinerated) and some is recycled.

We don't recycle very much at all! We really could do better! Can you think of any reasons why we shouldn't throw things away? Here are a few ideas:

- Making things from recycled material uses less energy and causes less pollution.
- Less valuable space is needed to get rid of waste.
- Less incinerators will be needed to burn waste.
- Less new materials need to be quarried or mined and less managed plantations need to be grown to make new things. This preserves valuable resources, natural habitats and wildlife.

- Many people do not like wasting things and would prefer them to be recycled.

So how can we stop all this rubbish? It's easy. All we have to do is remember the 3Rs – Reduce, Reuse and Recycle.

Top 10 waste tips at home . . .

1   Buy food with less packaging on. For example, instead of buying a pre-packaged four-pack of apples, buy them loose and put them in a paper bag. This will reduce the amount of packaging you will throw away and paper bags will also degrade more quickly than plastic bags. (Most local shops still use paper bags instead of plastic ones.)

2   Take your own shopping bag to the shop. This way you will reduce the amount of carrier bags you waste.

3   Don't use disposable things, for example:

Disposable Item	Alternative
Disposable nappies	Reusable cloth nappies
Disposable camera	Normal camera
Paper and plastic cups	China cup
Face wipes	Reusable flannel
Paper plates and plastic cutlery	China plates and metal cutlery
Paper serviettes	Reusable cloth napkins

Get recycling!

Information from Alupro

Get the recycling habit to help conserve the earth's resources and show your commitment to the environment, both globally and here in the UK. A lot of people doing something quite small to help the environment – makes a BIG difference!

And when you collect aluminium drinks cans and foil for recycling, you are not only helping the environment – up to 95% less energy is used every time a used drinks can or a foil pie case is recycled into new aluminium – but you are also releasing the high value of aluminium.

All over the country, aluminium cans and foil can be exchanged for cash, or donated to help raise funds for different local charities and community groups.

Or, you can give your aluminium to a local authority recycling scheme: most collect aluminium cans, and an increasing number operate foil schemes.

Every year in the UK almost 5,000,000,000 drinks in aluminium cans are consumed, along with foods packed or wrapped in 35,000 tonnes of aluminium foil. Over £10m a year is already paid to aluminium collectors, with another £30m-worth just waiting to be collected!

Exercise your options!

There are many opportunities for recycling aluminium across the UK – so check your local situation – and get recycling! Many places take both alucans and foil, but not all, so make sure you know what's right for you to collect locally. And remember that aluminium cans and foil must always be kept separate, as they are made from slightly different alloys and are recycled separately.

Use the value for good causes!

- Use one of over 500 Cash for Cans centres or mobile van sites to raise funds for charities, schools or other fundraising groups – or why not save to buy something for yourself?
- Give to local charities and community groups through special collection banks and schemes in many areas.

Support local authority recycling

- Most local authorities operate can banks, which collect aluminium drinks cans – and sometimes bags of clean foil – with steel food and drinks cans.

Many places take both alucans and foil, but not all, so make sure you know what's right for you to collect locally

- An increasing number of households can use a kerbside recycling service provided by their local authority, where different items such as cans, foil and newspapers can be put in a special container, which is then collected from your door.

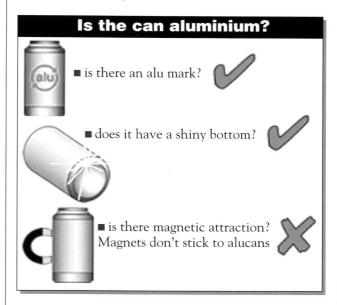

Is the can aluminium?

- is there an alu mark? ✔
- does it have a shiny bottom? ✔
- is there magnetic attraction? ✘
  Magnets don't stick to alucans

- The above information is from Alupro's web site which can be found at www.alupro.org.uk

© Alupro

Recycling rate 2001

	Tonnage Potential	Tonnage Recycled	Recycling Rate
Alucans	82,000	34,580	42%
Alufoil	26,000	2,990	12*%

The overall recovery rate for 122,000 tonnes of aluminium packaging, including aerosols, closures and barrels, is 34%.

Facts about recycling rate

- The recycling rate is for post-use aluminium packaging, as defined under EC packaging waste legislation.
- The recycling rate does not include the recycling of production scraps (such as the metal left when round foil containers are stamped from the foil reel). Quantities available, together with aluminium's high value, mean that this metal will nearly always be returned for recycling.
- The majority of aluminium packaging would be present in the domestic waste stream, if it were not diverted for recycling. Very little is available for collection through commercial waste systems.
- The term 'recovery' denotes the recovery of energy from waste where these facilities exist in an incinerator plant. Thin, food contaminated foil left in the waste stream will oxidise in an incinerator, releasing energy with the calorific value of coal.

* Alufoil is also recovered in energy from waste plants, adding 1,300 tonnes (5%) to the overall 16% recovery rate for foil

Source: Alupro

The recycling cycle

What happens to the glass that we put into the bottle bank? Where does it go?

Firstly, all unwanted non-glass materials are rejected then the collected bottles and jars are crushed into cullet (the industry's term for used glass).

The clean cullet is then sent to the glass container manufacturer where it is mixed and fed into a furnace with additional raw materials. The high temperatures involved in the melting process destroy any secondary decoration technique on the recycled glass such as paint and ink left in the mix. As the molten glass is drawn from the furnace it is channelled through a 'feeder' mechanism into the bottle-making machines.

Once the bottles have been formed they undergo a series of automatic inspection and quality control checks and are then sent to the filler. Once filled they are distributed to the retailer, and subsequently to the consumer with whom the cycle begins anew.

The quality of a recycled glass container is the same as the quality of the one which was first taken from the shelf at the beginning of the process. Recycled glass packaging is used in all market sectors from wine and beer to spirits and foods. Glass can be recycled indefinitely without any loss of quality.

Why recycle glass
There are five main reasons to recycle glass:

Reason One
Glass recycling cuts waste disposal costs. Glass makes up about 8% by

The quality of a recycled glass container is the same as the quality of the one which was first taken from the shelf at the beginning of the process

weight of our household refuse and any increase in the amount of glass recycled means savings on waste collection and waste disposal costs, which are likely to increase due to the landfill tax. It also extends the life of our landfill sites therefore conserving the British countryside.

Reason Two
Glass recycling saves energy. The amount of energy needed to melt recycled glass is considerably less than that needed to melt virgin raw materials to make new glass.

Reason Three
Glass recycling conserves the environment. Using recycled glass

in furnaces saves hundreds of thousands of tonnes of primary raw materials each year. This reduces the need for quarrying of raw materials and therefore conserves the countryside.

Reason Four
Glass recycling creates employment. A number of purpose-built recycling centres have been set up in the mainland UK to clean and process cullet. These centres provide employment and collection schemes also create local jobs.

Reason Five
Glass recycling increases public awareness of the problem of waste and the benefits of recycling. Each individual can play an active part in conservation by simply supporting bottle banking. This is a first step towards becoming an environmentally aware consumer.

■ The above information is from British Glass's web site which can be found at www.britglass.co.uk Alternatively see page 41 for their address details.

© British Glass Ltd

European glass recycling 2000

Country	National recycling rate
1. Austria	84%
2. Belgium	87%
3. Denmark	65%
4. Finland	84%
5. France	55%
6. Germany	83%
7. Greece	26%
8. Ireland	35%
9. Italy	40%
10. Netherlands	78%
11. Norway	85%
12. Portugal	40%
13. Spain	31%
14. Sweden	86%
15. Switzerland	91%
16. Turkey	24%
17. United Kingdom	29%

Source: Glass Gazette, FEVE

Return of the empties

Pop a deposit back on bottles, say ministers

By James Mills

A few decades ago it was a useful was for children to obtain money for a bag of sweets. Collecting empty bottles of pop to get back the deposit was a profitable venture for the youngsters.

Housewives could shave a few pence off the housekeeping budget by returning the family's empties each week.

The practice began to disappear more than 30 years ago but the Government wants to revive it to reduce the growing mountain of domestic rubbish.

With 30 million tons of household waste produced every year – a figure that is growing by 3 per cent annually – ministers are desperate to find ways to promote recycling.

Environment Minister Michael Meacher has asked officials to find ways that deposit schemes could work in modern Britain.

In the old days, the deposit was a penny or two per glass bottle. Now it would have to be at least 20p for there to be any incentive.

Critics said the reasons soft drinks companies scrapped the schemes still apply.

In the Fifties and Sixties soft drinks were produced and bottled locally, making them easy to return.

As national distribution centres became the norm, along with the advent of plastic containers and cans, this no longer made economic sense.

Now only 3 per cent of soft drinks are in glass bottles, and consumers are better off, making the small amount of cash less of an incentive than the pennies were to thrifty families who had lived through the war years.

Today's children – who aspire to expensive trainers and the latest mobile phone – are unlikely to return bottles, even at 20p a time, critics say.

The scheme still exists in independent shops in Scotland and a handful in England, but a

spokesman for the British Soft Drinks Association said: 'We believe these schemes are not the way forward.

'The main reason people don't return packaging is that it is inconvenient. The cash incentive is irrelevant.

Today's children – who aspire to expensive trainers and the latest mobile phone – are unlikely to return bottles, even at 20p a time, critics say

'The deposit would have to be enormous for people to think it was worth it.

'We want local authorities to provide better schemes to collect waste from homes for recycling.'

The dairy industry recycles bottles without the incentive of a deposit – customers simply leave the empties on the doorstep for the milkman. But more people are buying milk at the shops in cartons or plastic containers.

The Government is also considering charging households a 'rubbish tax' if they do not sort their plastic, glass and paper waste into separate bags for recycling.

Currently, 85 per cent of rubbish is sent to landfill sites. Only 7 per cent is recycled.

The Government wants to increase that to 25 per cent.

© *The Daily Mail, August 2002*

Glass recycling facts & figures

The 587,000 tonnes of glass recycled in the UK in 2001 saved 202,515,000 kWh of energy:
- That's enough energy to drive a car around the Earth 6,648 times
- That's enough energy to launch 10 space shuttle missions

- The 587,000 tonnes of glass is equal to 2.2 billion bottles and jars.
- Placed next to each other the containers would reach around the Earth four times
- Placed end-to-end the bottles and jars would reach to the moon and half way back
- Every household in the UK uses on average 331 bottles and jars per year.

The energy saving from recycling one bottle will:
- Power a 100 watt light bulb for almost an hour
- Power a computer for 25 minutes
- Power a colour TV for 20 minutes
- Power a washing machine for 10 minutes

If every household recycled all their glass bottles and jars then they would save enough energy to:
- Power a 100 watt light bulb for 12.5 days
- Power a computer for 5 days
- Power a colour TV for nearly 4.5 days, enough to watch 210 episodes of Coronation Street
- Power a washing machine for 2.5 days

© *Information from Glasspac, part of British Glass*

Cash for trash

You can make one adult-sized fleece jacket out of 17 used plastic bottles. But is recycling the answer to Britain's waste crisis? Emma Brockes investigates

The sticker on the hard hat says: 'Honk if you smell of wee'. It sits in a cubbyhole in the lodge of the Hurn Recycling Centre, Dorset. The men who work there stand on the line for nine and a half hours at a time, picking out contaminants from a stream of recyclable waste that shoots past on a conveyor belt. They don't, generally, have much to laugh about. The noise of the engines is too loud to talk over and, anyway, their mouths are covered by plastic masks. The only diversions from grimness are the sticker on the hard hat and a poster of Jennifer Aniston in a swimsuit, tacked to the back of a door.

Recycling schemes give their participants a sense of well-being that is not, for the most part, passed on to the people whose job it is to implement them. Recycling is dirty. After collection, the rubbish is dumped at a sorting centre. Then it's whizzed round an electrically charged belt that holds on to stainless steel, fires positive charges at aluminium cans, sending them into a separate bin, and senses through sophisticated computers the density of plastic bottles, identifying the adhesive on their labels and sorting accordingly. What is left flies past the hand-pickers in a cloud of evil-smelling dust.

The trick, they say, is to choose a spot at the back of the machine and keep staring at it, but even after taking this precaution if the conveyor belt stops abruptly, the men have been known to lurch to the ground with motion sickness. Their boss, Adrian Dufall, says: 'They're a good bunch of lads. It's a tough job.'

The recycling rate in this country is just over 9% (5% for commercial waste). In Germany, the figure is 46%, in Austria 45%, the Netherlands 44%, Sweden 35% and so on. The old thrift shop mantra, 'We turn your trash into cash', is not a simple equation. Green box collection schemes can cost between £85 to £175 per tonne (bottle banks and other bring-your-own systems tend to be much cheaper at £16 to £36). But the price at which most recycled materials are sold on is not enough to excite serious private sector investment. Matthew Gandy, author of *Recycling and the Politics of Urban Waste*, says that to the corporate waste industry recycling is little more than a 'red herring'. At Hurn, recycled paper fetches £30 a tonne; glass, between £22 and £27.50; PVC, £25. The only real money spinner is aluminium cans, which fetch £680 per tonne. They are so light, however, that Hurn only receives enough of them to make up one tonne per month.

Contamination is a constant problem. Wet newspapers can't be recycled and other bogus elements always work their way into the recycling stream and damage the batch. Consumers become infuriated as items acceptable for recycling chop and change – telephone directories and green wine bottles fall on and off the list. 'We like magazines,' says Dufall, 'because they use talcum powder and act as a water softener

when ground down.' He says it would be easier for his team if recyclable waste was separated at source, like in Denmark, where a three-bin system divides paper, glass and metals. Perishable waste goes for composting and the rest is landfilled or incinerated.

There never used to be a debate around recycling, because it was a natural part of the manufacturing process. Collecting scraps – rags, bones, old bottles – was part of the manufacturer's mandate and integral to production. Thriftiness was central to even wealthy householders' routines, or else the servants did it. In *The Philosophy of Dish-Towels*, published by *Good Housekeeping* magazine in 1885, readers were advised that 'No fragments of linen sheets or of damask table-cloths or napkins should ever be thrown away. If the pieces of linen are not large enough to make full-sized pillow cases, they may serve for children's pillows. The small bits that are impracticable for any other purpose, are admirable for steeping in liniment to lay upon a burn or wound.' Disposal of waste is now almost entirely separate from production. It is only through legal channels that the two are reunited: from 2005, manufacturers of electrical goods will be compelled by EU law to pay for the recycling of those products that people wish to dispose of.

There is innovation in the conversion of waste to usable materials. A factory in Slough makes fuel pellets out of the contaminated waste left over in recycling plants. Plastics can be turned into guttering and stockings. Shredded plastic makes fabric for sleeping bag wadding and fleeces. (It takes 17 bottles to make one adult-sized fleece.) But the only way to get people recycling in large enough numbers, seems to be to penalise them for not doing so. This week, Michael Meacher, the environment minister, floated the idea of putting a nine-pence tax on plastic carrier bags in an attempt to reduce the 'use them once and throw them away' culture. Eight billion carrier bags are used each year in Britain – that is 134 per head. The tax already exists in Ireland and has significantly reduced the number of bags swiped at the supermarket.

Other successful schemes tend to be those run by community, non-profit outfits. Worku Lakem runs a recycling round in Haringey, north London, which, he estimates, costs 10 pence per household, per week. For an average London borough of 200,000 homes, this comes to £1m a year, compared to £12m for refuse collection. The vehicle in which they collect the waste is a pedestrian-controlled buggy that costs seven pence a day to run and £8,000 to buy. The obstacle preventing more of these schemes taking off is local authority tendering requirements, which demand that companies prove they have sufficient assets to raise a performance bond of £1m. 'This,' says Lakem, 'has the effect of stifling competition and innovation.'

Shredded plastic makes fabric for sleeping bag wadding and fleeces. But the only way to get people recycling in large enough numbers, seems to be to penalise them for not doing so

---

The government has set a target of 25% of waste to be recycled by 2005, 16% by 2003. To those who work in the sector, this looks like an unfeasible figure unless people are given an incentive, penalised or motivated by a serious advertising campaign – like the ones for drink-driving – into doing more than lazily slinging refuse in a black plastic sack and imagining that their responsibility ends there. At Hurn, the men on the conveyor belt know better. For nine and a half hours a day, they suck up the dust and curse the consumer.

© *Guardian Newspapers Limited 2002*

Plastic bottle recycling

Did you know?

RECOUP

- A collection scheme for plastic bottles operates in 51% of local authority areas in the UK – 238 plastic bottle collection schemes.
- The UK now has over 4,140 plastic bottle banks and over 4.1 million households can have their plastic bottles collected as part of a kerbside collection scheme.
- Almost all plastic bottles are made from 1 of 3 types of plastic: PET e.g. fizzy drink bottles, cordial bottles, cooking oil bottles; HDPE e.g. milk and fruit juice bottles, washing up liquid bottles, fabric conditioner bottles; PVC e.g. still mineral water bottles, bottles for toiletries, cordial bottles
- PET bottles can be recycled to make a variety of end products, including fibre for sleeping bags and anoraks, new packaging, industrial strapping, wall and floor coverings, etc. Exciting new developments for PET include using the recycled material to make fleece clothing. It takes approximately 25 bottles to make 1 fleece jacket.
- HDPE bottles can be recycled to make a variety of end products, including fences, park benches and signposts. It can also be put back into bottles to be recycled again and again.
- PVC bottles can be recycled and used to make a variety of end products, including drainage pipes, electrical fittings and clothing.
- Recycling plastic bottles does make a difference – plastic bottle recycling cuts down on waste and saves energy. Recycling 1 plastic bottle saves enough energy to run a 60-watt light bulb for 6 hours.
- Did you know that you would need 20,000 plastic bottles to make a tonne?
- Recoup is the UK's national organisation for the recycling of plastic bottles. It is a non-profit making organisation, with charity status, which works with many plastic bottle recycling schemes throughout Britain.
- In 2001, almost 300 million (14,770 tonnes) plastic bottles were recycled in the UK. If all of these bottles were laid end to end, they would reach more than $7\frac{1}{2}$ times around the earth.
- Research has shown that if plastics were no longer used in packaging, the weight of packaging materials would rise by 300%, the volume of rubbish would expand by 150%, and the energy consumed by the packaging industry would increase by 100%.

- The above information is from a factsheet produced by Recoup. See page 41 for their address details.

© *Recoup*

plastic bottles
&
containers

Labour's 10p tax on plastic bags

By Thomas Harding

A tax on supermarket shopping bags in Britain seems certain because a report to the Government on Ireland's recent experiment is understood to recommend a levy of up to 10p.

A 10p tax on each disposable supermarket bag is likely to be among the first environmental policies recommended by Michael Meacher when he returns from the Earth Summit.

Shoppers in Ireland have reduced the number of bags they have been using by 90 per cent since the tax of 15 cents (10p) per bag was introduced in March.

Most Irish shoppers now keep their bags and reuse them. In Britain, only one in every 200 shopping bags is currently recycled.

An interim report on the first three months of the project has predicted that almost a billion plastic bags, one of the biggest litter eyesores, will be saved a year.

In Ireland, the tax windfall is to be used to set up an Office for Environmental Enforcement that will help to dispose of unwanted domestic fridges and freezers.

Confronted with paying 10p for their bags, Irish shoppers started recycling virtually overnight.

Latest figures from the first three months of the tax in Ireland show that bag usage by shoppers plummeted from an estimated 300 million over the three months to 23 million.

Martin Cullen, Irish environment minister, said: 'When one

> 'The fact that it is being looked at might suggest to you something.' With poor recycling, a large proportion of bags are thrown away, creating pollution problems

considers the scale of the litter problem caused by plastic bags in the past and the resulting cost of clearing them to the taxpayer, it brings home how this incentive has captured the public imagination.

'They have accepted the discipline of bringing their reusable bags with them when they go shopping.'

Before the legislation was introduced, about 1.2 billion bags were handed out to Irish shoppers without charge each year. In Britain, the figure is estimated to be 10 billion. Introduction of a bag tax for Britain's millions of shoppers is part of a fresh environmental approach by Labour.

When Mr Meacher ordered the Department of Environment, Food and Rural Affairs to look at the viability of a bag tax, he said: 'I would be arguing very strongly for putting something through here.

'Obviously, you have to talk about it with Government and get agreement but it is a cracking good idea.'

The tax will add about £28 a year to the average shopping bill of British households.

'The report is waiting to be looked at by Mr Meacher on his return,' a department spokesman said. 'The fact that it is being looked at might suggest to you something.' With poor recycling, a large proportion of bags are thrown away, creating pollution problems.

A whale, washed up in northern France last month, was thought to have died after mistaking plastic shopping bags in the sea for squid.

© Telegraph Group Limited, London 2002

The importance of paper recycling

Waste paper, or recovered paper as it is now often known, is the most important raw material for the British paper and board industry. Without it the industry would be less than half its present size and there would be consequential increased imports.

Reusing waste paper is good national housekeeping. Although fairly recently environmental concerns have led to more widespread public efforts to conserve and recycle resources, the paper industry has been recovering and re-using waste paper for over 100 years. This is not only because the 'urban forest' (waste paper) rather than the natural forest is the UK's prime resource but mainly because recycling paper makes economic and environmental sense. Two thirds of UK mills use recovered paper and many use nothing else.

© The Paper Federation of Great Britain

Uses of recycled waste paper

The following table shows different sectors' use of recovered paper in 1999:

Type of paper	UK production (000 tonnes)	Waste consumed (000 tonnes)
Newsprint	1090	1162
Printings and writings	1537	182
Corrugated case materials	1791	1900
Packaging papers	127	95
Household and sanitary	739	502
Others (inc. packaging boards)	921	690
Market DIP production		81
Total	6204	4612

Source: The Paper Federation of Great Britain

Issues

www.independence.co.uk

32

The green way to a garbage-free garage

Your loft is filled with half-used paint cans, you own several ancient mobiles the size of fridges – and an old fridge. Don't just chuck them out, says Jane Perrone – there is an environmentally sound answer. You make regular visits to the local bottle bank, recycle your newspapers and plastic bottles, and return plastic bags to your local supermarket. But what do you do when you want to get rid of more difficult items – computers, mobile phones and engine oil, for instance? The temptation is to chuck them in the dustbin. But the majority of things you throw away could be reused or recycled – and you could end up helping your favourite charity as well. Here are a few ideas to get you started:

Bicycles
Re-cycle collects and ships second-hand bikes rusting away in people's garages for rehabilitation and use in the developing world. (www.re-cycle.org)

Books
Rather than buying new books, you can buy and sell second-hand books from Green Metropolis. Once you've read them you can sell them back to someone else. (www.Greenmetropolis.com)

Alternatively, you can take old books to your local charity shop, or 'free' your book for someone else to pick up in a launderette, bus station or coffee shop, a principle invented by Book Crossing. That way you can find out what happens to your book, provided the finder bothers to email the website and let you know. (www.bookcrossing.com)

CDs
If you keep getting promotional CDs trying to sign you up for free ISP trials, you can use them as Christmas decorations, bird scarers or coasters. Unwanted music CDs will be gladly received by your local charity shop.

Computers
1.5m computers are dumped in landfill sites annually, according to computer recycling group Computer Aid (www.computer-aid.org) But these days there's no need to chuck your old computer in the dustbin when your spanking new top-of-the-range slimline laptop arrives. Computer Aid sends refurbished computers to the developing world. Computers for Charity (www.computersforcharity.org.uk) is one of the longest-established organisations that recycles discarded machines for community groups. Or try The Second Byte Project (www.2ndbyte.org), which donates computer systems to at-risk children.

Household appliances
Some charity shops accept electrical items in good working order; if you have a broken item, check the national recycling directory to find out whether your local council will recycle it for you. (Nt.Oneworld.Org/Wastewatch/Public/Index.Cfm)

Furniture
Don't buy new – recycle and renovate instead. (www.suite101.com/welcome.cfm/furniture_recycling)

Kitchen and garden waste
If you have a garden or an allotment, get a compost heap (www.compost.org.uk).If you don't have a garden, try a wormery. (www.greengardener.co.uk/worms.htm)

Mobile phones
These days there is no need to chuck your old mobile in the bin. A number of charities have recycling schemes, including Oxfam and Childline. (www.oxfam.org.uk www.childline.org.uk)

Environmental Mobile Control (www.emc-recycle.com) offers a free mobile collection and assessment service, raising money for Scope, Child Advocacy Inter-national and Samaritans Purse, while Cellular Reclamation Ltd (www.cellular-re.co.uk) raises money for Water Aid. Meanwhile a new scheme called Fonebak (www.foneback.com) claims to be the only phone recycling system that is in line with current and forthcoming EU recycling laws.

Oil
Dispose of old engine oil safely by taking it to a recycling centre. Plug your postcode into Oil Care (www.oilbankline.org.uk) to find your local depot.

Paint
If you're never going to use that tin of magenta gloss, why not check out Community Repaint (www.community repaint.org.uk) to find out if there is a paint reuse project near you. If not, check with youth clubs, schools and other local organisations in your area – they may be able to make use of it.

Plastic cups
Encourage your firm to recycle its vending machine cups. And bring in your own plastic cup instead of using the ones provided at the water cooler. (www.save-a-cup.co.uk)

Tools
If you have a garage or shed full of tools you never use, get in touch with Tools for Self Reliance (www.tfsr.org), which renovates them for use by workers in Africa.

Spectacles
Your old specs can be donated to Vision Aid. (www.vao.org.uk)

Toner cartridges
Many charities can turn toner cartridges into cash. Pick an organisation from Wastewatch's directory. (www.wastewatch.org.uk)

Did you know?

Your questions answered

The **PAPER FEDERATION** of Great Britain

Does recycling save trees?
No – it is inappropriate to talk in terms of whole trees as the papermaker generally uses the parts of the tree which other commercial users (such as builders and furniture makers) can't. That is the tops of the tree, saw mill waste and forest thinnings. This means that the tree would still be harvested even if the papermaker did not use the waste wood.

Can we recycle for ever?
Paper can only be recycled between 4-6 times, the fibres then wear out and lose their papermaking qualities. Primary fibre needs to then enter the chain to strengthen the fibres.

Are we depleting the world's forests to meet our demands for paper?
No. Great steps have been taken to ensure that forest levels are maintained. More trees are now being planted than are harvested.

Does the paper industry cut down tropical rainforests to meet the demand for paper?
Paper consumption has risen steadily over the past 20 years and it was all too easy to relate the growth in paper consumption to the destruction of the tropical rainforests.

Not surprisingly, the paper industry was offended at such suggestions and took every opportunity to refute the claim, pointing out as it did so, that tropical hardwoods were not used at all by the paper industry because they were unsuitable for papermaking.

This is no longer the case, mixed tropical hardwoods are being used in Indonesia to make pulp and paper from forests designated by the Government as suitable for conversion to plantations. These plantations will supply palm oil and rubber as well as woodpulp. The designated land may have been cleared by nomadic farmers to grow crops and then abandoned, or selectively logged for the most valuable species. As the conversion process takes place, the mixed hardwoods are being used to produce a general purpose mixed hardwood pulp that will be used in the production of printing and writing papers. In time acacia from the plantations will be used to produce high quality uniform fibres that will be used in printing and writing papers.

Are paper mills polluting river water?
Stringent regulations are applied to the water which paper mills return to rivers. Paper makers recycle the water they use and it is very often the case that it goes back into the river cleaner than when it came out!

Do we use too much paper?
Paper has many natural attributes which make it a very attractive material to use: it comes from a naturally renewable source; it is recyclable and it is biodegradable.

The amount of paper used has certainly increased, and this is partly due to developments in technology which have made paper suitable for many more purposes than originally imagined. Paper plays a very important role in everyday life. However, it is easy to take it for granted but, like all the world's resources, paper should never be used thoughtlessly or wastefully. Common sense should prevail.

Don't use more paper than you need for the purpose. Whenever possible, recycle your paper once you have finished using it.

Is it better to recycle, to incinerate or to landfill?
After use, paper can end up going down any of these three routes. The most economic and environmentally responsible route is recycling, although there is a practical limit to the amount of waste paper that can be recycled. Once recycling requirements have been met, incineration is the next preferred option, especially as this can produce energy. Landfill is the least favourable option

■ The above information is from the Paper Federation of Great Britain Information Centre's web site which can be found at www.ppic.org.uk

© *The Paper Federation of Great Britain*

Making compost

Information from the Young People's Trust for the Environment

Why make compost?

The kitchen and garden waste that you throw in the bin ends up either being burned or being dumped in landfill sites.

BUT . . . it can be recycled and made into compost!

What is compost?

Kitchen and garden waste is made up of organic matter. When you leave dead organic matter in a heap for a few days it will start to rot. Rotting is caused by bacteria, algae and fungi which eat the soft succulent bits of waste. All this eating makes them hot and encourages them to multiply. More heat and more bacteria mean that the organic matter is broken down more quickly. Organic matter is made up of anything that is, or was once alive.

Worms and beetles then eat the larger bits of waste. By the time all this is finished you are left with a dark brown crumbly mixture which is called compost.

Make a compost heap

How to start

A compost heap can just be a pile of kitchen scraps and garden waste. To speed up the rotting process, however, you can do several things.

Neat and tidy!

To keep your heap neat, you could make a wire mesh bin from chicken wire and four posts . . . You don't have to use chicken wire – wood or plastic sheets could be used instead.

Where to put it

Compost heaps like warmth, so, if you can, find a spot in your garden which is sheltered from the wind and in a sunny position. Remember compost heaps need to be damp but not waterlogged. Putting a piece of

What can you compost?

grass cuttings
hay
hedge trimmings
paper (with no coloured ink)
vegetable peelings
straw
tea bags
leftover vegetables
fruit

old carpet, wood or some newspapers on top helps keep out the rain.

Top tip!

If you line your compost bin with old cardboard or carpet it will keep it warm and damp – ideal conditions for bacteria to work in!

■ The above information is from the Young People's Trust for the Environment's web site: www.yptenc.org.uk

© *Young People's Trust for the Environment*

Your clothes

Information from the Salvation Army Trading Company Limited

You recycle paper to save trees
You recycle cans to save resources
You recycle glass to save energy
But clothing seems to pose a problem. Yes, you often fill the 'charity' bag when it comes through the door, or sometimes take items to the charity shop or even pass around 'hand me downs'. But still over 7.5 billion articles of clothing end up in the nation's dustbins every year. It just doesn't make sense, especially when you think that on average these clothes still have more than 60% of their useful wearable life left in them and our clothing banks are only operating at approximately 25% capacity, so . . . why not recycle clothes . . . to save people.

Your benefits

These are legion.
■ The environment is damaged less – clothes in landfill give off noxious gases and some take a long time to rot.
■ People benefit all over the world as they are provided with jobs and thus the wherewithal to purchase clothing at prices they can afford.
■ The UK national and local economies receive a 'shot in the arm' as many 100s of regular fully recompensed jobs are created nationwide.

At the moment 75% of recyclable clothes are wasted. You can make the difference

---

■ The income the Salvation Army receives helps to fund beds for the homeless, cups of tea for the thirsty, food for the hungry, comfort for the lonely, sick and deprived, and much, much more . . .

At the moment 75% of recyclable clothes are wasted. You can make the difference.

Your future

Fundamentally there is the need to galvanise ourselves into a new mindset where waste minimisation and recycling become second nature both in the home and workplace.

Sustainability is a buzzword these days, but there is a lack of awareness that the way in which an item of clothing can be recycled, begins at the design stage. There is a need, therefore, to stimulate the designers of tomorrow to create clothes which can easily be worn again and again but, when finally finished with, can be more readily recycled into 'new items'.

Simply put, sustainable development means ensuring a better quality of life for everyone, both for today and for future generations, but translating this philosophy into a reality will require that the general public as well as the experts understand what contribution will be required of them.

We must all realise that we have a hidden resource that can be used to provide efficient business opportunities that can help protect the environment and improve lives. Have you caught the vision? Want to know more? Then go to www.textilesonline.org.uk

What happens to my clothing?

When you place your unwanted clothes into a Salvation Army Clothing Bank, a complex, but well-organised, process is started. A local collector empties the clothing bank at least once a week. He firstly offers the clothes to the local Salvation Army Officer to help those less fortunate in your area. Secondly, some items are offered for sale through local Salvation Army charity stores. Garments which can't be used locally are transported, by 40 foot trailer, to our purpose-built facility in Wellingborough. The clothing is then sorted. The wearable clothes go to help people in the UK, Central Africa, Pakistan and the Baltic States. The unwearable items are either re-spun, used as wiper cloths or as mattress filling or sound proofing. In all over 90% will be used, somewhere, somehow by someone.

Help lines
Sometimes problems occur, a bank may be full, accidentally something is dropped into the bank, someone may have damaged it in some way. If you have received a plastic bag through your door, occasionally it may not be collected or you may have another query then use the Help Line number below, leave a message and contact phone number and we will do the rest.

For Clothing Banks only call 0845 458 1999 (calls are charged at local rates).

For Door to Door Bag collections only call 0845 458 1812 (calls are charged at local rates).

Don't forget your shoes:
In addition to clothing we also need ladies', gents' and childrens' footwear.

■ The above information is from the Salvation Army Trading Company's web site which can be found at www.tecweb.com
© Salvation Army Trading Company Limited

Clothing waste

The size of the problem

- 900 million items of clothing are sent to landfill sites each year.
- 6% of the average household bin is made up of used clothes.
- Only 2% of the British public recognise that recycling textiles is an important thing to do.
- 80,000 tonnes of old clothes and other waste textiles are dumped in bins during the Christmas period alone.
- All clothes put into recycling banks are sent to factories where they are sorted. The condition of the clothes we put in the banks is important – if they are wet and dirty, they can contaminate a whole batch.
- Most of the clothes collected by the Salvation Army are sent to Africa and the Indian subcontinent.
- There are around 3,000 clothes recycling banks scattered across the UK. Organisations benefiting from recycled clothes are the Salvation Army, Oxfam, SCOPE and the British Heart Foundation amongst others.

Assistant Chief Executive Barbara McPhail commented: 'We dump nine hundred million items of clothing into the waste stream each year and that is extremely damaging from an environmental point of view. The fact is, if these clothes are in a reasonable condition they could be worn by those more unfortunate than ourselves, or sold to fund important social projects.

So dumping used clothes in a domestic bin just doesn't make sense. We'd like this situation to change, and given the facilities and encouragement to recycle – I'm sure British people will respond.'

To back up the media messages, ENCAMS launched a poster campaign, which was seen on Adshel bus stop sites and billboard posters around the country, with the cheeky slogan 'Drop your pants . . . off at one of our banks'.

Before the campaign launch in January 2002, ENCAMS worked with the Salvation Army, the Textile Recycling Association and councils throughout Britain, to try and station as many recycling banks as possible in accessible places. This has resulted in a huge increase in the number of clothing banks, with 47 councils siting new facilities in their area. To track down the success of the initiative, the Salvation Army weighed donated clothes from their clothing banks pre- and post-campaign.

So after the publicity and the hype, was the campaign a success? ENCAMS and the Salvation Army are very pleased to announce that it was, with a verified 24% increase in clothing donations.

■ The above information is from ENCAMS' *Annual Review 2001-2002*. See page 41 for their address details.
© ENCAMS

Energy from waste

Frequently asked questions

Did you know?

- The contents of an average dustbin in one year could be used to produce enough electricity for you to watch TV for 5,000 hours or enough heat to take 500 baths or 3,500 showers.

- The waste of five million Parisians provides the Paris District Heating Company with 43% of its needs – enough to heat 198,000 apartments.

- Many Energy from Waste (EfW) plants produces steam to drive turbines which generate electricity. One such plant in Amsterdam produces 15% of the city's electricity.

- Sometimes heat from EfW plants can be used to dry sludge or distil water for industrial use. The EfW plant in Rotterdam produces electricity and distils over six million cubic metres of water per year.

- Combined heat and power plants are common in Germany and Scandinavia where it is estimated that the annual waste of seven households can supply the complete annual heat and power needs of one whole household.

Does EfW discourage recycling?

No. It is entirely complementary when properly planned, and EfW power stations are sized to allow scope for recycling to develop, and use combustibles that do not lend themselves to recycling. Member States with a strong record of recycling also utilise energy from waste as a complementary waste technology.

Is it true that EfW is not required because recycling will increase?

The success of recycling relies on the cleanliness and quality of the material, and good source segregation in the home. The availability of secondary markets for the recycled materials is also an important driver of the recycling industry. But if

materials are contaminated or dirty, recycling is not cost effective. Even if materials are ideal, with landfill becoming scarcer – due to physical and political reasons – there is the need for other treatment methods to divert as much as possible from landfill. Recycling alone cannot provide the answer.

Are local populations at risk of ill health from incinerators?

There are ever more stringent controls of atmospheric releases and lower emissions than ever before. For example, the UK Department of Health has reported than since 1990, emissions of lead from EfW plants have dropped by 97% and of dioxins by 99%.[1] Older non-compliant incinerators are either being phased out or will be upgraded to be in compliance with the EU Incineration Directive.

Is there a future for landfill?

There will always be the need for managed landfill conforming to the

---

The contents of an average dustbin in one year could be used to produce enough electricity for you to watch TV for 5,000 hours

---

EU Landfill Directive 1999/31/EC. Both recycling and recovery processes inevitably create small amounts of waste resulting from their industrial processes. However, the amount of landfill capacity needed will decrease as witnessed already in some EU countries where landfills are closing or strict limits are being placed on capacity.

Surely plastics should be recycled rather than incinerated?

While plastics recycling is a growing industry, a portion of plastic waste cannot be sensibly recycled. In addition, plastics are almost all derived from oil which is already used to generate power. The APME[2] estimates that if all the EU plastic waste which is not feasible to recycle were turned into energy, it would be equivalent to at least 17 million tonnes of coal. This would represent 15% of the total EU coal imports and approximately 5% of EU energy needs for power generation.

References

1 *Dispelling the Myths*, The Energy from Waste Association, October 2000.
2 Association of Plastics Manufacturers in Europe

- The above information is from a factsheet produced by ASSURRE, see their web site at www.assurre.org
© ASSURRE

Weighing the evidence

'Ecoteams' are learning how to cut waste and reduce fuel use

By Simon Birch

Over the past seven months, Sue and Trevor Clayton have become avid weight watchers. Each week they have had the scales out anxiously, hoping that they have shed an extra pound or two. However, the couple from the Nottinghamshire village of Flintham have not been focusing on their waistlines, but on the amount of waste they have been discarding.

As members of the Flintham Ecoteam programme, the Claytons have been taking part in a pilot project in the Rushcliffe district, with the support of the local council and the green charity, Global Action Plan.

Made up of between six and eight households, the goal of each Ecoteam is to improve the environmental performance of individual households.

Over a seven-month period, a team works together, with the help of a coach, to reduce the impact of daily life upon the environment.

Each month, the team look at a different topic: waste, gas, electricity, water, transport and shopping, and discuss how practical changes around the home and to their lifestyles can benefit the environment. The success of these changes is monitored by weekly checks of the gas and electricity meters and by weighing the amount of rubbish produced by each household.

'People are genuinely overwhelmed by the enormity of the environmental crisis,' says project coordinator Penney Poyzer. 'What we do is break it down into manageable, easy actions.'

Conceived in the US more than 10 years ago, the Ecoteam programme has been a great success across north America and throughout Europe, particularly in the Netherlands, where more than 10,000 families have been through the programme.

The project was brought over to Nottingham by a Dutch national, Karina Wells, who had become an enthusiastic advocate of Ecoteams. 'It's important to bear in mind that little changes can add up to make a big difference,' she says.

The changes that the Flintham Ecoteam has undertaken have all been easy to implement. For example, Jenny Lennon describes one of the ways she has been able to reduce the amount of gas that her family uses. 'We now try to use just one pan to cook with, and use this to steam other things, plus we try to cut down the amount of food we cook in the oven,' she says.

Other ways in which the group has saved energy range from putting reflector boards behind their radiators to improve efficiency, to turning down the thermostat on the central heating by just a couple of degrees.

Often these practical tips are nothing more than common sense. 'We've saved electricity simply by not keeping the video or hi-fi on

stand-by,' says 16-year-old Jack who, along with his 12-year-old brother Tom, has been representing the Reacher family at the Ecoteam meetings. 'You also get into the habit of switching off lights in rooms, even if you think you'll be back in 10 minutes,' adds Tom.

Some of the most dramatic results have come from the amount of rubbish the Ecoteams have managed to save. 'Before we started the programme, we'd fill nearly three large bin bags a week,' says Sue Clayton. 'Now we've managed to bring that down to just one.'

The Claytons now recycle all their plastics, cardboard, paper and glass, as well as composting their organic waste. And to reduce the amount of packaging, Sue now buys loose fruit and vegetables rather than pre-packaged.

While the Flintham figures are still being compiled, the experience of other Ecoteams suggests that, on average, each household reduces its rubbish by 50%, water consumption by 22%, gas by 17% and electricity by around 10%.

'As well as an environmental incentive, there's also a financial benefit,' says Poyzer, 'as each household saves around £200 due to reduced energy use and car use.'

She believes the key to the Ecoteam programme is the way in which people learn good, life-long environmental habits. 'Essentially, what we achieve is behavioural change, and this is crucial if we're going to get people to respond positively and practically to the environmental message,' she says.

'We'll definitely continue,' says Sue Clayton. 'Once you get into the habit, it becomes second nature.'

Rushcliffe district council is now keen to extend the project across the whole area.

■ The Ecoteam programme can be contacted on 0115-9143893.

The big clear-up

Radical proposals for waste disposal

By Joanna Collins

The government and many local authorities are in a deep hole over waste. With the amount of household rubbish set to double by 2020 to over 40m tonnes a year, and new European directives insisting that Britain significantly reduces its landfilling, the incineration option looks attractive, but is proving politically and financially difficult.

The government, which is currently conducting a full waste review, suggested last week that householders who do not recycle their rubbish would have to pay up to £1 a sack to have it removed. It hints that radical change is coming, but, in the meantime, many local authorities around the world are turning to a system called zero waste that would abolish landfills and reduce dramatically the need for incinerators.

Getting rid of waste altogether sounds pie in the sky, but is, in fact, quite simple. The premise is that everything we buy is, or eventually will be, made from materials that can be repaired, reused or recycled. So governments, councils and industry should be working together to find ways to turn waste into a profitable resource or designing it out of the system altogether.

Canberra, Toronto, California and, lately, New Zealand – where 45% of all local authorities have signed up to zero waste policies – are convinced enough to make it a target to be reached by 2015 or earlier. The UN and the South African government have agreed to green the Johannesburg summit by following zero waste principles.

Now the initiative has been picked up by Sue Doughty, Liberal Democrat MP for Guildford, who recently launched a charter and 10 commandments that call on government to get rid of household waste by 2020. 'Councils are required to be financially risk-averse,' she says, 'so without government setting enabling regulations they don't have the empowerment to go as far as they might'.

But Bath and North-east Somerset council is not waiting on government; it is the first authority to have adopted the zero waste vision. Colchester and Braintree councils, in Essex, are now following.

Getting rid of waste altogether sounds pie in the sky, but is, in fact, quite simple

'Zero waste is, to me, a grassroots movement from local authorities and people,' says Bath councillor Roger Symmonds. He was won over to the concept two years ago at a conference in Geneva, where New Zealand authorities that had taken the plunge recounted their experience. 'Don't get too hung up on the zero bit,' he cautions. 'It may not be achievable. But if we get anywhere near, then the benefits for health and jobs will be enormous.'

The early signs are good. Where Britain currently recycles 11% of household waste, burns 8% and dumps the rest, within six years of a change in policy Canberra is re-cycling 59% of its rubbish and Edmonton, Canada, has reached 70%.

Surprisingly, organic waste makes up the bulk of a bin-load and causes the nastiest health risk when it rots and leaches from landfill. Composting, according to the cities which have adopted zero waste policies, can immediately reduce the problem. In many cases, the high achieving cities and councils have introduced three-stream collection, separating organics, dry recyclables such as bottles and plastics, and tricky residuals such as batteries.

According to Robin Murray, a leading zero waste economist, as soon as this is done 'they find suddenly that they are recycling more than 50%'.

There's money to be made, too, say the zero waste proponents. In a recent US survey of high recycling programmes, savings were made in 13 out of the 14 cases. Resource recovery facilities and exchange networks were found to be turning waste into an asset, creating small business opportunities and employ-ment in struggling communities.

This has been a key factor in New Zealand, where zero waste is regarded more as a driver of local economic development than a matter of environmental conscience. 'It's very much a case of the people led and the government followed,' says Warren Snow, of the New Zealand Zero Waste Trust. 'It's a quiet revolution where non-profit community groups are turning waste into jobs.'

Radical thinking about waste is seen to be essential. When it comes to the 15-20% of waste that is difficult or expensive to recycle, zero waste proposes a new way of looking at the problem: anything that cannot be recycled or reused should be designed out of the system. Here, industry is seen as a key player. 'The multi-nationals are on to this far quicker than governments or environmental groups', says Murray. Many large companies, he says, already foresee the arrival of legislation that makes producers take responsibility for what happens to their products at the end of the life-cycle.

■ Together, we produce around 27 million tonnes of household waste in the UK every year. That's a massive half a tonne per person. (p. 1)

■ Each year 22 million tonnes of household waste is dumped in landfill sites. (p. 1)

■ During 1999/2000 over 26 million tonnes (an average of almost 500kg per person) was collected by local authorities. Just over 10 per cent of this waste is recycled or composted. (p. 2)

■ Every year in the UK we use 13 billion steel cans which, placed end to end, would stretch to the moon – three times! (p. 4)

■ If all the aluminium cans sold in the UK were recycled, there would be 12 million fewer full dustbins each year. (p. 5)

■ The UK sends 26% of its tyres to landfill, far less than some other EU countries. France sends almost half, Spain 58%, but Holland sends none. (p. 8)

■ Local councils spend about £332 million every year cleaning litter from streets in Britain. (p. 9)

■ According to the pest control industry, the amount of rodent infestations has grown by 24 per cent over the last two years. (p. 11)

■ Estimates put the amount of rubbish dropped per year in 1964 at five million tonnes. By 2001, that figure was above 25 million tonnes. (p. 11)

■ In the majority of Beachwatch beach litter surveys over 50% of the litter recorded is made from plastic. (p. 13)

■ Globally, an estimated one million birds and 100,000 marine mammals and sea turtles die every year from entanglement in, or ingestion, of plastics. (p. 13)

■ Each year, Britain throws away 435 million tonnes of rubbish, of which 106 million tonnes is household waste. The majority goes into landfill sites. (p. 15)

■ The dangers of landfill are manifold: they release toxic gases such as methane, carbon dioxide, hydrogen sulphide and vinyl chloride into the air, old batteries buried deep within the sites leak poisonous metals into the ground water. (p. 15)

■ Around 80% of household waste could be either recycled or composted, dramatically reducing the need for landfill. (p. 16)

■ Britain's record of 11% recycled household waste is a quarter of its northern European neighbours. By 2016 EU law will force Britain to cut the 80% of its waste going to landfill down to 33%. (p. 17)

■ Glass is completely recyclable yet we throw away 1.5 million tonnes of it a year. (p. 22)

■ Only 14% of the glass used in Britain is recycled compared with 37% in Germany, 50% in Switzerland and 29% in Europe as a whole. (p. 22)

■ At present less than 25% of the paper in use is recycled and the rest is produced from wood pulp. (p. 23)

■ Make your own compost. On average, 20% of our household waste consists of organic matter such as vegetable and fruit peelings, tea and coffee grounds. (p. 24)

■ Every year in the UK almost 5,000,000,000 drinks in aluminium cans are consumed, along with foods packed or wrapped in 35,000 tonnes of aluminium foil. (p. 27)

■ The UK now has over 4,140 plastic bottle banks and over 4.1 million households can have their plastic bottles collected as part of a kerbside collection scheme. (p. 31)

■ Research has shown that if plastics were no longer used in packaging, the weight of packaging materials would rise by 300%, the volume of rubbish would expand by 150%, and the energy consumed by the packaging industry would increase by 100%. (p. 31)

■ Shoppers in Ireland have reduced the number of bags they have been using by 90 per cent since the tax of 15 cents (10p) per bag was introduced in March. (p. 32)

■ A whale, washed up in northern France last month, was thought to have died after mistaking plastic shopping bags in the sea for squid. (p. 32)

■ 900 million items of clothing are sent to landfill sites each year. (p. 36)

■ Only 2% of the British public recognise that recycling textiles is an important thing to do. (p. 36)

■ The waste of five million Parisians provides the Paris District Heating Company with 43% of its needs – enough to heat 198,000 apartments. (p. 37)

■ The amount of household rubbish set to double by 2020 to over 40m tonnes a year. (p. 39)

Issues Online

Subscribe to our six new **Issues** titles each term on a firm sale basis and you gain free online access to information from each of the books in the **Issues** series. And each term we add the information from the latest six **Issues** titles to the web site. On receipt of your order, we will send you your user name and password for your 20-user free licence. Of course you may cancel your subscription to **Issues** at any time under no obligation, but this would also cancel your free online subscription.

To find out more, visit our web site at: www.independence.co.uk/news

Independence Educational Publishers
PO Box 295
Cambridge, CB1 3XP
Tel: 01223 566130

ADDITIONAL RESOURCES

You might like to contact the following organisations for further information. Due to the increasing cost of postage, many organisations cannot respond to enquiries unless they receive a stamped, addressed envelope.

Aluminium Packaging and Recycling Organisation (Alupro)
1 Brockhill Court
Brockhill Lane
Redditch, B97 6RB
Tel: 01527 597757
Fax: 01527 594140
E-mail: info@alupro.org.uk
Web site: www.alupro.org.uk

ASSURRE – The Association for the Sustainable Use and Recovery of Resources in Europe
av. E. Mounier 83 box 5
B-1200 Brussels
Belgium
Tel: + 32 2 772 52 52
Fax: + 32 2 772 54 19
E-mail: management@assurre.org
Web site: www.assurre.org

British Glass
Northumberland Road
Sheffield, S10 2UA
Tel: 0114 268 6201
Fax: 0114 268 1073
E-mail: recycling@britglass.co.uk
Web site: www.britglass.co.uk

Bureau of International Recycling (BIR)
24, rue du Lombard – bte 14
1000 Brussels
Belgium
E-mail: bir.sec@skynet.be
Web site: www.bir.org

The Chartered Institution of Wastes Management
9 Saxon Court,
St Peter's Gardens
Marefair
Northampton, NN1 1SX
Tel: 01604 620426
Fax: 01604 621339
E-mail: technical@ciwm.co.uk
Web site: www.ciwm.co.uk

ENCAMS (Environmental Campaigns)
Elizabeth House, The Pier
Wigan, WN3 4EX
Tel: 01942 824620
Fax: 01942 824778
E-mail: information@encams.org
Web site: www.encams.org and www.encams.org/citizenship

Friends of the Earth (FOE)
26-28 Underwood Street
London, N1 7JQ
Tel: 020 7490 1555
Fax: 020 7490 0881
E-mail: info@foe.co.uk
Web site: www.foe.co.uk

Global Action Plan (GAP)
8 Fulwood Place
Gray's Inn
London, WC1V 6HG
Tel: 020 7405 5633
Fax: 020 7831 6244
E-mail: all@gappuk.demon.co.uk
Web site: www.globalactionplan.org.uk and www.ergo-living.com

Greenpeace
Canonbury Villas
London, N1 2PN
Tel: 020 7865 8100
Fax: 020 7865 8200
E-mail: gn-info@uk.greenpeace.org
Web site: www.greenpeace.org.uk

Industrial Council for Packaging & the Environment (INCPEN)
Suite 108, Sussex House
6, The Forbury
Reading, RG1 3EJ
Tel: 0118 9253466
Fax: 0118 9253467
E-mail: info@incpen.org
Web site: www.incpen.org

Marine Conservation Society
9 Gloucester Road
Ross-On-Wye, HR9 5BU
Tel: 01989 566017
Fax: 01989 567815
E-mail: mcsuk@mcmail.com
Web site: www.mcsuk.org

The Paper Federation of Great Britain
Information Centre
Papermakers House
1 Rivenhall Road,
Westlea
Swindon, SN5 7BD
Tel: 01793 889663
Fax: 01793 886182
E-mail: ppic@paper.org.uk
Web site: www.ppic.org.uk and www.paper.org.uk

Recoup
9 Metro Centre
Welbeck Way
Woodston
Peterborough, PE2 7WH
Tel: 01733 390021
Fax: 01733 390031
E-mail: enquiry@recoup.org
Web site: www.recoup.org

Salvation Army Trading Company Limited
66-78 Denington Road
Denington Industrial Estate
Wellingborough, NN8 2QH
Tel: 01933 441086
Fax: 01933 44549
E-mail: office@satradingco.org
Web site: www.satradingco.org

Waste Watch
96 Tooley Street
London, SE1 2TH
Tel: 020 7089 2100
Fax: 020 7403 4802
E-mail: info@wastewatch.org.uk
Web site: www.wastewatch.org.uk

Young People's Trust for the Environment
8 Leapale Road
Guildford, GU1 4JX
Tel: 01483 539600
Fax: 01483 301992
E-mail: info@yptenc.org.uk
Web site: www.yptenc.org.uk

INDEX

aluminium recycling 2, 4, 22-3, 27, 30

beach litter 13
bicycles, recycling 33
biodegradable plastics 22
books, recycling 33

cans, recycling 22, 23, 27, 30
cars
 disposal of car tyres 7-8
 scrap 7
CDs, recycling 33
clothes, recycling 35-6
composting waste 18, 19, 21, 22, 33, 35, 39
 making your own compost 24-5, 35
 worm composting 21, 24, 25
computers, recycling 33

dams, and hydroelectric power stations 23
dioxins 6, 8

Earth Summit (Johannesburg 2002) 15
Eco Schools 9, 20
Ecoteam programme 38
electrical appliances
 disposal of 7
 recycling 33
ENCAMS Fast Food Code of Practice 12
energy production
 Energy from Waste (EfW) plants 19-20, 37
 and incinerated waste 6, 17, 19-20, 37
energy saving
 and the Ecoteam programme 38
 and glass recycling 29
Environmental Mobile Control 33
Environmental Protection Act (1990) 9, 10, 11
European Union (EU)
 and fridge disposal 7
 landfill directive 1, 6, 15, 17, 37, 39
 recycling legislation 14

fast food litter 11, 12, 21
fridge disposal 7, 14, 17
Friends of the Earth 3, 16, 25
furniture, recycling 33

glass recycling 4, 5, 21, 22
 centres 28, 30
 energy saved by 29
 process of 28
 re-use of ground glass 18
 returnable bottles 22, 29
 statistics 29
Global Action Plan 5
Greenpeace 6

household waste
 alternatives to disposable items 20-1
 amounts of 2, 3, 15, 17
 charging for the disposal of 17, 18, 39
 clothing 36
 composition of 1, 2
 and the Ecoteam programme 38
 and energy production 37
 and the EU landfill directive 1
 Government policies on 14, 15, 16, 17, 20, 29, 39
 kerbside collections of 17, 18, 24
 and packaging 15, 20, 22, 25
 recycling 4, 5, 16, 17, 20, 21, 22-3
  changing attitudes to 30-1
 tips regarding 20-1, 25
 see also composting waste
hydroelectric power stations 23

INCPEN (Industry Council for Packaging and the Environment) 10-11
industrial waste recycling 23
Ireland, recycling in 14, 15, 31, 32

landfill sites 1, 15, 16, 19, 29
 and car tyres 7-8
 clothes in 35, 36
 EU landfill directive 1, 6, 15, 17, 37, 39
 future of 37
 and glass 28
 methane emissions from 1, 3, 5, 15, 24
 old computers dumped in 33
 and organic waste 1
 and paper 34
 problems for local communities 3
 UK compared with other countries 18
 and zero waste policies 39
litter 9-13
 causes of 10
 clearing up 9, 10-11
 dangers of 9
 and the law 9, 10
 marine litter 13
 and packaging 10
 plastic bags 32
 public attitudes to 9
 and rats 11-12

marine life, and tyre reefs 8
marine litter 13
metals, recycling 22, 26
mobile phones, recycling 33

oil recycling 23, 26, 33
organic waste 1, 2
 composting 18, 19, 21, 22, 39
  making your own compost 24-5, 35
 recycling 5, 22

Issues   *www.independence.co.uk*

42

ACKNOWLEDGEMENTS

The publisher is grateful for permission to reproduce the following material.

While every care has been taken to trace and acknowledge copyright, the publisher tenders its apology for any accidental infringement or where copyright has proved untraceable. The publisher would be pleased to come to a suitable arrangement in any such case with the rightful owner.

Chapter One: The Problems of Waste

Waste – what's the problem?, © Crown copyright is reproduced with the permission of Her Majesty's Stationery Office, *Household waste and recycling*, © DEFRA, National Assembly for Wales, CIPFA, *Top 10 wacky waste facts!*, © Waste Watch, *The mess we're in!*, © Friends of the Earth, *Waste facts*, © Crown copyright is reproduced with the permission of Her Majesty's Stationery Office, *Waste*, © Global Action Plan (GAP), *Annual waste arisings by sector*, © Crown copyright is reproduced with the permission of Her Majesty's Stationery Office, *The problem with incineration*, © Greenpeace, *Fridge mountain could cost £40m*, © Guardian Newspapers Limited 2002, *Dumped on*, © Guardian Newspapers Limited 2002, *Litter*, © Eco-Schools, *The litter issue*, © The Industry Council for Packaging and the Environment (INCPEN), *Time to cut back on the rat pack*, © The Chartered Institution of Wastes Management, *Materials recycling through local authority schemes*, © Crown copyright is reproduced with the permission of Her Majesty's Stationery Office, *Marine litter*, © Marine Conservation Society, *EU drive on recycling 'too fast' for Britain*, © Guardian Newspapers Limited 2002, *Rubbish! That's our recycling record*, © Guardian Newspapers Limited 2002, *Waste arisings and management*, © Crown copyright is reproduced with the permission of Her Majesty's Stationery Office, *Government must tackle waste crisis*, © Friends of the Earth, *Britain's abysmal record*, © Guardian Newspapers Limited 2002,

Estimated annual waste in the UK by sector, © Crown copyright is reproduced with the permission of Her Majesty's Stationery Office.

Chapter Two: Reducing Waste

Waste minimisation, © Eco Schools, *What is waste?*, © Crown copyright is reproduced with the permission of Her Majesty's Stationery Office, *Top 20 waste tips*, © Waste Watch, *Recycling*, © Young People's Trust for the Environment, *How to recycle*, © Crown copyright is reproduced with the permission of Her Majesty's Stationery Office, *Recycling top tips*, © Friends of the Earth, *The role of recycling*, © Bureau of International Recycling, *Get recycling!*, © Alupro, *Recycling rate 2001*, © Alupro, *The recycling cycle*, © British Glass Ltd, *European glass recycling 2000*, © FEVE, *Return of the empties*, © The Daily Mail, August 2002, *Fast facts*, © British Glass Ltd, *Cash for trash*, © Guardian Newspapers Limited 2002, *Plastic bottle recycling*, © Recoup, *Labour's 10p tax on plastic bags*, © Telegraph Group Limited, London 2002, *The importance of paper recycling*, © The Paper Federation of Great Britain, *Uses of recycled paper*, © The Paper Federation of Great Britain, *The green way to a garbage-free garage*, © Guardian Newspapers Limited 2002, *Did you know?*, © The Paper Federation of Great Britain, *Making compost*, © Young People's Trust for the Environment, *Your clothes*, © Salvation Army Trading Company Limited, *Clothing waste*, © ENCAMS, *Energy from waste*, © ASSURRE, *Weighing the evidence*, © Guardian Newspapers Limited 2002, *The big clear-up*, © Guardian Newspapers Limited 2002.

Photographs and illustrations:

Pages 1, 6, 10, 14, 17, 24, 26, 37: Simon Kneebone; pages 3, 8, 34: Pumpkin House; pages 15, 25, 38: Bev Aisbett.

Craig Donnellan
Cambridge
January, 2003